model
professionals

The "Topical Times" Premiership Eleven — and they're all less than three inches high!

CORINTHIAN's football figures have been an astounding success, with over 10 million sold to over 2.5 million collectors. It won the coveted "Best New Toy Range 1996-97" at the British Association of Toy Retailers awards.

The 7 cm high models are initially sculpted from a current photograph of the player by one of 11 full-time sculptors. The figures then go through a stringent quality control to ensure that exceptional player likeness is achieved. They then go back to the sculptors for alterations (if needed) then all the facial features are hand painted and the body finished in the correct home strip. The fully painted original is then forwarded to the respective football club for approval. Either the football club approves the model, or in some instances the actual players approve their own models. The authorised models are then sent back to Corinthian from the clubs and are shipped off in this fragile form to their factory to have the moulds made for the final figurines. All figurines are then produced in the factory and hand painted (by one of the 4000 full-time painters) to include all the necessary details including club badge, sponsors' logo, player's name and squad number on the back of their authentic home strip. They are then shipped in their fully finished state back to the UK, ready to hit all the stores.

CORINTHIAN have also released similar figures from the worlds of rugby, basketball and cricket.

This is our Premiership Eleven, but with hundreds of figures to choose from you could easily make up your own team . . . or teams!

FERGUSON

Turn to page 126 for The "Topical Times" Team in real life!

£5.25

conte

the topical times football book

4

6. **SIMPLY THE BEST** Peter Schmeichel (Manchester United)

10. **HOMING INSTINCT** David Batty (Newcastle United)

12. **POWER-HOUSE** Jason McAteer (Liverpool)

14. **AERIAL WARFARE**

16. **THE PRICE ISN'T RIGHT** Muzzy Izzet (Leicester City)

18. **BOSS MAN** David Platt

20. **FIRM FAVOURITE** Alan Stubbs (Celtic)

24. **QUIZ**

25. **HOME INTERNATIONALS** Riccardo Scimeca (Aston Villa)

28. **MARATHON MAN** Steffen Iversen (Spurs)

30. **SHORT CHANGE** Craig Short (Everton)

32. **FRANK TALKING** Frank Leboeuf (Chelsea)

36. **LATE STARTER** Per Pedersen (Blackburn Rovers)

38. **SCREENPLAY!**

43. **CITY SLICKER** Darren Huckerby (Coventry City)

44. **BACK TO THE BIG TIME** Nigel Martyn (Leeds United)

46. **SPECIAL EFFECTS**

48. **TOUR OF DUTY** Lee Bradbury (Portsmouth)

50. **LONDON SCOTTISH** Neil Sullivan (Wimbledon)

52. **SECONDS OUT** Billy Dodds (Aberdeen)

56. **DREAM DEBUT** — 4 page picture story.

62. **DANNY'S BOY** John Hendrie (Barnsley)

64. **TEN OF THE BEST** Alan Shearer (Newcastle United)

69. **ALL IN A DAY'S WORK**

72. **MIDFIELD MAGICIAN** The Glenn Hoddle Story

76. **THIRD TIME LUCKY** Mark Crossley (Nottingham Forest)

78. **CHAMPION JOCKY!** Joachim Bjorklund (Rangers)

82. **WHO'S THE BOSS?** Ian Brightwell (Manchester City)

84. **FULL HOUSE**

86. **FOOTBALL FOOTBALL**

88. **LOCAL HERO** Jon Newsome (Sheffield Wednesday)

90. **GETTING EVEN**

92. **PAST MASTERS**

97. **CROSSWORD**

98. **IT'S A FUNNY OLD GAME!**

100. **THANK DEVON** Dean Sturridge (Derby County)

104. **ROLLER COASTER RIDE** Craig Hignett (Middlesbrough)

107. **HOME WINS** Jamie Pollock (Bolton Wanderers)

108. **THE WONDER OF WEMBLEY**

113. **COUNTY PRACTICE** Alun Armstrong (Stockport County)

116. **HOME DRAWS** Ian Bishop (West Ham United)

119. **WHO'D BE A REF?**

120. **AND TODAY'S TEAMS ARE . . .**

122. **THE WEMBLEY WAY** Carlo Nash (Crystal Palace)

simply the best?

Manchester United keeper PETER SCHMEICHEL refuses to accept he's better than all the rest!

SINCE his arrival at Old Trafford in the summer of 1991, success has never been more than a long throw away from goalkeeper Peter Schmeichel.

During that spell, the Manchester United keeper has helped his club to win four Premiership titles and two FA Cups.

His performances were also inspirational as his country, Denmark, won the European Championships in 1992.

The giant Dane has set goalkeeping standards so high that he is regarded in many quarters as the best keeper in the world.

It is an accolade which he is reluctant to accept and, ironically, one for which he would never have been considered had his coaches not stuck him between the posts at the age of nine simply to keep him out of harm's way and prevent him from being a danger to the other players. But for that decision, he would never have considered becoming a goalkeeper. In fact, he only played football because his friends played the game.

Says Peter, "When I first started, I never thought much about what position I would play. I didn't actually have much of a clue about football. I just played in the street along with the rest of the kids and we made up our own rules as we went along.

"I watched football on television, but didn't really understand the game. Even as a teenager, when I had been playing as a goalkeeper in organised matches for several years, I did not understand the offside rule.

"Everybody else shouted for offside, so I did too. But I hadn't a clue what it meant."

Consequently, when he turned up

at his local club at the age of nine, asking for a trial, he was as naive about the game as it is possible to be.

"The football set-up for boys in Denmark is different to the way things are done in England," he explains. "You can just go along and join your local professional club and if you develop well enough, you may eventually play for them in the national league.

"If Manchester United was a Danish club, all the kids who support them could just go along and sign up as a player.

"Clubs like Brondby, for instance, have youth teams with three or four thousand members.

"When I was nine, I just turned up at my local ground because everybody else did.

"At that age, I was the same size as all the other boys of my age. I think I was about 14 when I took off in size.

"Nevertheless, I was a bit too wild to play outfield. I used to charge around and dive in recklessly.

"The coaches decided I was too

dangerous to the rest of the players, so they put me in goal. I've been there ever since.

"Fortunately, I liked playing in goal straight away. It suited my temperament to be able to dive around the penalty area. I also happened to be very good at it, as my coach, team-mates, their parents and my own parents kept telling me.

"At that age, when people tell you things like that, you believe them and, as time went on, the more compliments I received, the more ambitious I became.

"By the time I was in my teens, people were telling me that I would become the best in Denmark and would play for my country and I believed them.

"Around that time, we started to produce some fantastic players in Denmark.

"In 1977, Liverpool played against Borussia Moenchengladbach in the European Cup Final and Allan Simonsen scored a fantastic goal for the German side.

"For his contribution to his club and country that season, he was voted European Footballer of the Year, the only Danish player who has won the award.

"That opened my eyes and made me think, 'I'd like to do that.'

"I moved to Brondby from my first club, Hvidovre, when I was 24 and, at one point, started to take it for granted that I would end up playing for one of the big clubs in Europe.

"Even then, I was wanted by a number of clubs throughout Europe, who could have paid me much more than any Danish club could have paid at the time, but none of them were among the elite of the Continent.

"I decided I would rather play for Brondby and be in Europe every year, so I could be where the national coach could watch me regularly and I could also concentrate on doing well for Denmark.

"I think that was one of my better

Continued over page

decisions. We ended up in the semi-finals of the UEFA Cup, played extremely well and were unlucky not to go to the Final.

"In terms of my own development, I think it was important to have taken part in that, instead of leaving Denmark and maybe not being ready to join a bigger club.

"By the time, I joined Manchester United, I had known about their interest for nearly two years. The first year was a long wait, wondering if they would follow up their interest with an offer.

"At the end of 12 months, they came up with an offer, but Brondby's asking price was too high and I was devastated.

"I was forced to wait another year and was very angry with Brondby for making this happen. I thought their valuation of £1.2 million was unfair. Seven years ago, that was a huge fee for a goalkeeper.

"So I stayed, Brondby went to the UEFA Cup semi-final and United won the European Cup-Winners' Cup. That summer, I finally joined them."

Schmeichel is pleased to report that his goalkeeping standards have improved with each year at United, but when pundits describe him as the best in the world, he plays down that judgment.

"Although I know I am a good goalkeeper, there is no way I would ever claim to be the best in the world, even though some people have hung that label on me," he goes on.

"It is such a false title. Only one player who was ever tagged the best in the world deserved that title and stayed there for much of his career. That was Diego Maradona. Nobody ever disputed his right to have that title.

"Take my own position during the European Championships staged in England in 1996, for example.

"During the first week of the tournament, I was being touted by many people as the best goalkeeper in the world. Then, in our second match, I played for Denmark against Croatia. We lost 3-0 and the next morning I was no longer the best in the world.

"How can your status change in a few days? That is why I do not accept

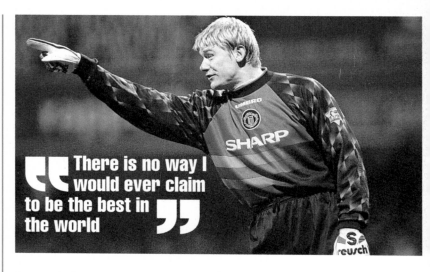

> There is no way I would ever claim to be the best in the world

the tag. As long as your manager knows your qualities and trusts in your ability, that is all that matters."

Last season, Schmeichel was as reliable as ever during United's quest for another Championship while also chasing glory in the European Cup.

Schmeichel's flamboyant, demonstrative style has also given him a reputation as one of football's most controversial characters. It is his way of dealing with the pressures of playing for England's most-watched club.

He says, "This is not a club where every good player in the world could come and play well. There is always so much pressure, you must be strong to deal with it.

"When I came here, I joined a team full of mega-stars. Then, five of them disappeared. Just like that, new names had to be built up and I started to receive a bit more attention. Suddenly, I was one of the big stars of the team.

"Every player who has made a bit of a name for himself here has experienced the same thing. There is nothing you can do about it. You cannot escape the spotlight, so you just have to go along with it.

"I know that everything I do on the pitch will be closely monitored and every mistake I make will be a big celebration for some people.

"I think every United player is in the same boat. But, in my position, I am closest to the fans and the easiest target. I'm in the area all the time, so I am easy to insult.

"I am no longer shocked by the things which some fans shout at me. I have always had the attitude that opposing fans must never get to me and make me commit mistakes. I simply would not allow that to happen, so I have built up a defence system against it.

"You would not believe the abuse which comes my way sometimes. But I have never been tempted to give it back.

Every mistake I make will be a big celebration for some people

"I know exactly what would happen if I did. I would be reported and land in trouble with the football authorities. But I am thick-skinned and turn the other cheek."

Peter's mental strength has given him the concentration levels required to keep him sharp and alert — an essential asset when playing at the top level.

"My concentration always has to be at a peak for the 90 minutes I am on the pitch," he explains. "It is always a big part of a goalkeeper's game, and it is the way I have played all my life.

"I have always played for the best team in its league, so I have become used to enduring long, quiet spells. But I always keep on my toes and make sure I am always involved in the game, no matter where the ball is.

"I have my own techniques for doing that. For instance, you will always see me well out of my goal, shouting and giving directions.

"I know that, most of the time, the rest of the team can't hear me, but by acting in this way, I feel that I am in the game and that I have a say in it.

"It is important for me to be like that, because I am not the sort of goalkeeper who can stay in his box, just stand there and look at the game.

"I know that has led to me being given the 'Mr Angry' tag but, then, so many things which have been written about me are not true. So I just ignore it because I am really not interested." ●

ARSENAL patrick VIEIRA

dAVID BATTY and Alan Shearer were arguably the two most important signings made by former Newcastle United manager Kevin Keegan.

The £19 million required to tempt the pair from Blackburn Rovers has been money well spent — and much appreciated by their former boss at Ewood Park, Kenny Dalglish, who inherited them when he took over following Keegan's resignation at the start of 1997.

Shearer's goals and Batty's steadying influence in midfield have given Newcastle the type of reliable service which drove Blackburn to the Championship in 1995.

By adding Batty and Shearer, Newcastle's natural flair has been bolstered by the sheer professionalism which typified Blackburn in their title year. There are no sideshows with the two England men, just value for money.

Newcastle believe the title-winning experience of the two men will prove invaluable as the club chase silverware. Batty, however, who won his medal at Leeds but refused one at Rovers because he did not feel he had played often enough to merit it, does not believe that past success makes a shred of difference.

David admits, "I think it is a myth when people say that you need players who have won things in order to win a Championship. I don't think Alan and I have made any difference to the attitude of the rest of the lads since we came here.

"We have both won the Championship before we came here, but I don't play any differently just because I have won the title and I don't think Alan does, either.

"What we both do is just get on with our jobs. My attitude and approach is the same for every game I play, whether it is a reserve game or an international.

"I have always been like that throughout my career and have never approached one game differently to another. Maybe that is the secret to playing well. If you go out and forget about the importance of a game, you won't get nervous.

"When I won the League with Leeds, only John Lukic had previously won a medal. Blackburn won it with only myself and Bobby Mimms having previous title experience and we only played seven games between us. The lads at Newcastle are well capable of winning something, even without Alan and me.

"This is the best team I have played in. When we have been at our best, it has been better than any side I have been involved in at Leeds or Blackburn. I don't think I have played in a better team, even when I have been with England!

"I have become a better player in my time here and that says it all. No specific aspect of my game has improved. I just feel that, by playing alongside such good players, my game is flourishing.

"Despite what some people may think of me, I enjoy playing

> **I enjoy the hard work and getting stuck in as well, but I'm a passing player and Newcastle play the way I like it.**

real football with the ball on the floor. I enjoy the hard work and getting stuck in as well, but I'm a passing player and Newcastle play the way I like it.

"I am allowed to play my natural game. Nobody has ever pulled me to one side and told me how he wants me to play."

Over the past year, Batty has regained his England place and rediscovered the form he displayed prior to the serious foot injury he sustained at Blackburn three seasons ago.

The injury kept him out of the game for nearly a year, but he still draws on that experience, even though he is back to his best.

David goes on, "I appreciate what I have now. I have had a bad injury and like every player who has been through a similar lay-off, you realise that you can

be finished in the game in no time.

"Things are going well for me at the moment, but I know that even a little twist on the training pitch can finish you. During my injury lay-off, I promised myself that I would enjoy every day once I was fit again and that's what I am doing.

"I was aware of the injury for a while after I returned because it was still quite sore. I haven't had any problems since, but I have to touch wood when I talk about it.

"I feel little twinges now and again, but I think any player who has had a serious injury will say the same. You just have to take more care of yourself.

"I like to keep everything on an even keel and I still live in Wetherby, despite leaving Elland Road four years ago. I was used to a long trek when I played for Blackburn, but a drive of just over an hour to Newcastle makes it seem like it is just around the corner!

"It is about a 150-mile round trip, but the club has been fair to me and I think I have been fair to myself.

"If the travelling ever proved too much, I would have to be honest and work out a solution because I wouldn't be doing myself or the team justice.

"My family means everything to me and I wouldn't uproot my wife, Mandy, and young twins, Jack and George, just for the sake of it. If the travelling ever became too much, I would have to consider things very carefully.

"I think it helps to be based away from where I play. I can get away from it all at home. I still don't know how fanatical the Newcastle fans are because the only time I am there is when I am working.

"I have never been shopping in Newcastle. I can imagine that it could be horrendous at times. The fans love you and they live for football, but I like to get away from it. I never went into Blackburn when I wasn't working.

"As long as my family are happy, so am I." •

INSTINCT

power-house!

That's JASON McATEER, Liverpool's pocket dynamo!

ASON McATEER realised every Liverpool fan's dream when he arrived at Anfield from Bolton Wanderers for a £4.5 million fee in September 1995. Born in Birkenhead to Liverpool-mad parents, Jason was never going to be anything other than a devoted follower of the Reds.

That is why past achievements, such as playing at Wembley in a Coca-Cola Cup Final and experiencing the 1994 World Cup Finals with the Republic of Ireland, paled into insignificance alongside the day that he put pen to paper on a Liverpool contract.

Two years on and the thrill of being a Liverpool player has yet to fade. He still cannot believe how lucky he is.

Being a Liverpool fan and player has, though, become something of two-edged sword for the right wing-back. He has become a potential liability.

Indeed, Liverpool's hunt for the top honours is under threat — because McAteer loves the club just too much!

He explains, "Sometimes I let my enthusiasm run away with me and don't concentrate as well as I should. It is just that I want to do well for the club.

"The biggest problem comes when we go a goal down. I'm so desperate to get us back in the game that I start to do things that I shouldn't.

"Instead of carrying on with the

> **It doesn't matter what time in a game the opposition score, I've still got the energy to get forward. When that and my enthusiasm mix, it can be dangerous.**

things that I'm good at, I try too hard to get the goal back.

"I should hold my position and keep the team's shape, but sometimes I get carried away and bomb forward too much. That can leave a nice hole for the opposition to exploit.

"The manager, Roy Evans, has talked to me about it. It isn't a matter of losing my head, I just have to calm down a little.

"Roy has told me to keep things simple, help the team retain possession and wait for an opportunity to arise. I can be guilty of trying too hard to make things happen.

"We always create

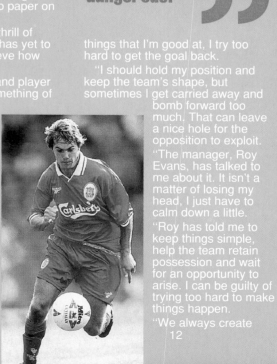

chances at Liverpool and, if I do the right things, a chance will come along and we will equalise. It sounds simple, but I still find it hard to stay so calm.

"I am a Liverpool fan and always will be and I still think like one at times.

"There aren't many at the club who have supported the club since they were kids. The likes of Steve McManaman and Robbie Fowler were both Everton fans before coming to the club.

"Because I wasn't tied to a club at an early age, I was able to come to Anfield as a fan.

"I feel very, very disappointed when we lose. Every player does

but, as a fan as well as a player, I find defeat particularly hard to take.

"I can sympathise with how the fans feel after a defeat because I feel just like them.

"I'm made very aware of how the supporters think because my whole family are fans of the club. I can't get away from it.

"When I was at Bolton, there weren't that many requests for tickets because it was a bit far out for friends and family. As soon as I joined Liverpool, though, requests immediately went up.

"Everyone wants to talk to me about the club and I can get carried away by it all.

"I want to do so well for the club, my family, friends and myself."

It is a problem not helped by Jason's renowned fitness levels.

He explains, "It doesn't matter what time in a game the opposition score, I've still got the energy to get forward. When that and my enthusiasm mix, it can be dangerous.

"If I see possibilities and I'm not concentrating properly, I feel I can use my energy to exploit them. I should really be thinking of the consequences when I do that.

"I've always had a good 'engine'. I was hyperactive as a kid, the kind of youngster mothers hate.

"I was always under my mother's feet and she used to hate me being in the house. She used to boot me out.

"I suppose she was trying to tire me out. It never worked.

"In the long run, it has helped me to develop a good 'motor'. I just have to make sure I don't use it at the wrong time.

"It wasn't a problem at Bolton because I was a box-to-box midfielder and was encouraged, basically, to do what I wanted and cover every blade of grass.

"I was a young lad and I don't think the management wanted me to be burdened too much with team responsibilities.

"At Liverpool, I have to think more about the team. That is what is preached more than anything at Anfield.

"I can't go and bomb forward all the time. I have to channel my enthusiasm in the right way.

"Manager Roy Evans has said that he doesn't want to take the drive from my game. He recognises that enthusiasm can be a good thing and he doesn't want me to lose that.

"A couple of seasons ago, in the FA Cup semi-final against Aston Villa, I scored deep into injury time precisely because I was still 'up' for the game. Not many people can say they have scored on such an occasion and I did so because of my enthusiasm.

"What I intend to do is to be mentally stronger and concentrate. That, I've been told, will come with experience and age so, hopefully, it won't be a problem for too much longer."

aerial

JON NEWSOME, Sheffield Wednesday v. COLIN COOPER and NIKOLA JERKEN, Nottingham Forest.

STEVE WALSH, Leicester City v. MARK HUGHES, Chelsea.

ALF INGE HAALAND, Notts Forest v. MICHAEL DUBERRY, Chelsea.

STEVE BOULD, Arsenal v. JASON DODD, Southampton.

CARLTON PALMER, Leeds United v. DAVID HILLIER, Portsmouth.

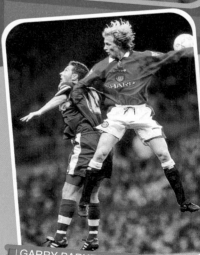

COLIN HENDRY, Blackburn Rovers v. DARREN ANDERTON, Spurs.

GARRY PARKER, Leicester City v. JORDI CRUYFF, Manchester United.

14

warfare

GRAHAM STUART, Everton v.
JASON McATEER, Liverpool

EMERSON and CURTIS
FLEMING, Middlesbrough v.
GIANLUCA VIALLI, Chelsea.

LEICESTER CITY'S Muzzy Izzet has already pitted his wits against the international superstars gracing the Premier League.

Yet the talented midfielder has had to sit back and watch his dreams of a call-up to the Turkish World Cup squad disappear, and all because he refused to sign a piece of paper.

East-End born Muzzy joined Chelsea as a youngster but sprung to prominence in 1996 during a loan spell at Filbert Street when he helped the East Midlands side win promotion at Wembley in the play-off final.

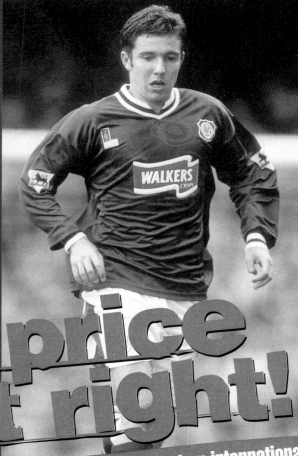

the price isn't right!

Why Leicester City's MUZZY IZZET missed out on international football

His non-stop displays and infectious enthusiasm left Leicester manager Martin O' Neill in no doubt that the loan deal should be turned into a permanent move.

Muzzy was delighted to make the switch from London to Leicester and things looked even better when he was all set to make his international bow after finding out he qualified to play for the Turks due to his father's Turkish-Cypriot background.

However, despite the excitement and anticipation of playing on the international stage, Muzzy now realises that he was only one signature away from spending three months in the Turkish army.

Muzzy explains, "I first found out about the Turkish interest in April, 1996. We had just won a

crucial home match against Birmingham, and as I was getting changed after the game I was handed a card that someone had left for me at Filbert Street's reception area.

"I couldn't believe what I was seeing when I opened the card up to find out that it was from a representative of the Turkish Football Association and he was waiting upstairs in the Gary Lineker Suite to talk to me.

"We met and he told me they had researched my family background, watched me for a couple of weeks, and wondered if I would be interested in

> **Basically there was no way I was going to sign something I couldn't read, so I asked for a translation.**

playing international football for Turkey.

"The representative left me with that proposal and promised me he would get back to me at a later date.

"Sure enough, when the season had finished, we'd

won promotion and I'd signed for Leicester he contacted me again and asked me to go down to the Turkish Embassy in London.

"I arranged an appointment to sort out the dual Turkish/British passport I qualified for, and needed to have, in order to play for them. That was when the problems began.

"When I arrived at the Embassy I was given a form to fill in, but I couldn't understand a word because it was all in Turkish. My father and grandparents speak Turkish, but I've lived in London all my life and I don't understand a word!

"Basically there was no way I was going to sign something I couldn't read, so I asked for a translation.

"I was stunned when an official told me that the form was a declaration order that would mean a three-month spell of national service with the Turkish army if I signed.

"The embassy officials tried to reassure me that a loop hole would be found to keep me away from the army, but I wasn't convinced and told them they would have to put that in writing before I signed anything.

"That was when they lost interest because I haven't heard anything since, which is an obvious disappointment because I really thought I was in with a realistic chance of playing a part in Turkey's World Cup qualifying campaign.

"In fact, when I first heard of their interest the Euro '96 squads had not been announced. The thought of playing in that tournament was unbelievably exciting for somebody who hadn't started many more than 10 first team games.

"Ironically, after everything that happened I ended up watching the Turkish games on television in a hotel bar whilst on holiday in ...Turkey!"

WEST HAM UNITED

michael HUGHES

boss man!

LOOKING for a football manager of the future? David Platt's your man.

The former England captain looks a natural to take over a hot-seat when he hangs up his boots or earlier if he's offered a player-manager's job.

It was when he was playing for Serie A side Sampdoria in Italy that Platt started to think about the idea that one day he might become the boss. By the time he came back to England to join Arsenal in 1995, he was already thinking ahead.

"I've worked with some great managers in my time and I've learned something different from all of them," says David. "That doesn't mean I've agreed with everything they've done, of course.

"But because I'm looking to stay on in the game as a manager, it's important I store as much information away as possible. For that reason, I've kept a close eye on all my managers at both club and international level, here and in Italy.

"I've no idea what sort of manager I'll make. That's something I'll have to find out if and when I get the chance.

"It's definitely a move I want to make one day. As a player I wanted to play abroad and as a manager I'd like to sample every aspect of the job.

"Of course, it would be good to be in charge of a really big club and be able to go out and buy some of the players I know. In the long-term, I'd also be keen to really prove myself by managing on a shoe-string at a smaller club.

"It all depends on when I decide to give up playing and when a job offer might come my way. There are a couple of years left on my contract at Arsenal and when that ends I'll have to make some sort of decision.

"Only then will I know if I could take on a player-manager's job. That's a tough task to combine the two.

"Italy's where I really started to get my ideas together about management. Although I was only 25, I realised the years were flying past and I would have to look to the future.

"My Swedish manager, Sven Goran Eriksson, made a big impression on me at Sampdoria. I'm sure there are several aspects of his approach to the game I'd use myself as a manager.

"Eriksson puts his ideas across so well to the players. It was through his ideas that he gained the respect of those players, which is a key issue for any manager.

"He knew how to treat players properly. Win, lose or draw, he would never lose control after a match.

"His style was to come into the dressing-room and shake everybody's hand whatever the result. The time for talking about it was the next day in training.

"I thought he was a superb manager. I'm sure he would have done well in the Premier League if he hadn't turned down the Blackburn Rovers job.

"Foreign coaches are starting to make a big impression on the game here. The players came first but now clubs are starting to realise that there are some top-class managers in Europe as well.

"Ruud Gullit and Arsenal's own Arsene Wenger both had great first seasons in charge in the Premiership. I'm sure there will be more to come in the years ahead.

"Arsene was intelligent enough to open players' minds first before he made dramatic changes. He has his own methods but he wanted to get the

> I've no idea what sort of manager I'll make. That's something I'll have to find out if and when I get the chance.

■ ARSENE WENGER

■ SVEN ERIKSSON

important things right first.

"There was no point in telling experienced players they had to do things completely differently. More radical ideas could be introduced once he'd got himself established.

"The players at Arsenal knew the score. The likes of Tony Adams, Lee Dixon, Steve Bould and David Seaman have done it all before and that's seen the club through any problems in the past.

"At the start of last season everybody thought the club was in crisis when Bruce Rioch left five days before the start of the season. But English players are very resilient and we didn't let it bother us.

"When Arsene Wenger finally took over, the team were already going well. That gave him a strong base to build on.

"Continental coaches and managers all have to get used to the way things are here in England. There are far more games for a start.

"That makes it very difficult for coaches to plan training because there's no rest between games. People say that English footballers need to train more but when are we supposed to do it?

"In Italy, where they play from Sunday to Sunday, they can use that time to train properly for the next game. They know exactly what they're going to do every day.

"Here in England it has to be very different. If you have a very hard midweek game, you can't do anything the next day.

"The body needs time to recover. Over-playing doesn't help anyone.

"These are all problems I'd face as a manager. I look forward to that challenge." ●

FAVOUR

Celtic's ALAN STUBBS

ALAN STUBBS knew exactly what joining Celtic would mean — after witnessing a former RANGERS star play his heart out in a FRIENDLY against Tommy Burns's men!

Scouser Stubbs avidly followed Everton throughout his youth, and coudn't resist going along to Goodison Park to see his heroes take on Celtic in Neville Southall's testimonial match.

Alan expected a small band of Scottish supporters to be in the ground, and anticipated the usual slow, easy-going atmosphere for what was basically a friendly match.

Instead, he had his eyes opened by a passionate display by Toffees' hero, Duncan Ferguson, who played against his former Old Firm foes as though it was the most vital game of his career.

"I realised what the Old Firm was all about when I saw how much big Dunc was putting into that match," Alan recalls.

"Despite having left Rangers and Glasgow behind, he was desperate to put one over on his old rivals, and he had a great game.

"But Celtic, too, showed that there is no such thing as a friendly for them — especially against an ENGLISH side!

"They attacked throughout and put on an exciting display — and they brought a huge, amazing support with them, who gave Neville Southall a brilliant reception.

"I remember thinking, 'I woudn't mind playing for this lot', and it's funny to think how things worked out and I did end up at Celtic Park."

Normally a modest, laid-back character, Stubbs shows that even he has been bitten by the Old Firm bug — which means for most fans in Glasgow, you're either a Celt or a 'Ger.

"The critics have been going on all season about how hard Rangers' German star, Jorg Albertz, can hit a free-kick," Alan explains.

"But I've been trying to persuade manager Tommy Burns to let me try my luck at OUR set-pieces. They say Big Jorg's shots reach around 80 miles-an-hour, and I reckon mine are even HARDER!

"But, seriously, I thrive on tough, competitive games, and the Old Firm derbies are something else. The old red mist was coming down over my eyes in the last one at Ibrox, when Andy Goram and Ally McCoist were both having a go at me, but it's a unique fixture!

"I'm convinced both clubs are big enough to more than hold their own against the top English Premiership teams — and hopefully we can prove that if and when a British Cup or League is started.

"In the meantime, every match we play against Rangers is like a Cup Final — and don't forget that every other side plays out of their skins when they face the Old Firm!"

After Southall's testimonial, Alan didn't take much convincing when Celtic approached Bolton Wanderers for his signature. And he duly became the Hoops' record signing at £3.5 million.

But perhaps he jumped at Celtic's offer partly because he had already suffered a transfer trauma — when he came agonisingly close to signing for another Celtic legend, Kenny Dalglish.

"Blackburn came in for me and my Bolton team-mate, Jason McAteer, when Kenny was manager there," Alan recalls, "and I would have signed just on the strength of his huge reputation.

"Kenny won everything with Celtic and Liverpool, and I believed Jason and I would be guaranteed success working with him and Chairman Jack Walker's millions.

"What I didn't realise was that Jason had also spoken to Liverpool and, when Rovers found out, they made it clear they only wanted the two of us as a package — I wouldn't be going to Ewood Park on my own.

"I was really gutted after that, but I was still sure the right move would come along if I just waited. I'm pleased to say that happened when I eventually made my move to Celtic!"

Laid-back Stubbs claims being the Bhoys'

> I thrive on tough, competitive games, and the Old Firm derbies are something else

…TE

…nas caught the Old Firm bug!

record signing hasn't added to the pressure on him to succeed, but he admits his first full season brought its fair share of personal disappointments.

For the first time in his career, injuries left him sidelined on several occasions, and the likeable Scouser admits it couldn't have happened at a worse time.

"I'd always been very fortunate in the past, and was hardly ever forced to sit out games," he explains ruefully.

"So, when I picked up my first knock at Celtic, it was a new experience for me. I reckon any player returning from injury needs six or seven matches to get near to full fitness again.

"And the worst problem was MYSELF, because I

came back too soon. Maybe I thought the supporters would start wondering if I had been worth all that money.

"But hurrying back just meant I was more prone to picking up ANOTHER injury, and the whole thing

made the season very unsettled for me — the fans have definitely still to see me at my best."

On a brighter note, Alan's former Bolton team-mate John McGinlay — a dyed-in-the-wool Celts fanatic — claimed that Tommy Burns had just signed England's next skipper when he brought Stubbs to Glasgow.

That hasn't transpired yet, but those injuries didn't help Alan's chances of grabbing Glenn Hoddle's attention, ahead of proven thoroughbreds like Tony Adams, Stuart Pearce, Gary Pallister and Sol Campbell.

So, while he isn't expecting an international call-up immediately, Alan is happy to admit he's still hopeful of one day pulling on the famous white shirt

at Wembley.

"It's still a dream for me, and I am still optimistic that it can happen one day," he reveals. "That would be the pinnacle for me.

"Realistically, there is a lot of tough competition for places in the England defence, but I'd like to think Glenn is keeping up-to-date on how I'm doing.

"As Celtic — and everyone else in Scotland — continue to buy top-quality foreign players, I'm being given a harder test almost every week, and I'm also learning from my own team-mates.

"I know I am not the finished article, but I am playing at a good level, and that can only help my cause. However, Celtic pay my wages, and they come first." ●

21

COVENTRY CITY gary **McALLISTER**

michael GRAY

QUIZ time

1 What will be unusual about the 2002 World Cup?

2 From which club did Chelsea sign Gianfranco Zola?

3 Who scored his first international goal for England last season against Mexico?

4 Which teams knocked Manchester United out of the Coca-Cola Cup and FA Cup last season?

5 Why will Kenny Dalglish be unique if Newcastle win the Premiership this season?

6 Who is the odd one out — Nicky Butt, Gary Neville, David Beckham, Phil Neville or Paul Scholes?

7 Which Premier League club increased their average attendance in every one of the last six years?

8 Which country failed to turn up for a World Cup qualifier against Scotland?

9 Why did a Premiership match cost Middlesbrough five points last season?

10 Who knocked Liverpool out of last season's European Cup-Winners' Cup?

Question 12

11 Name the only two strikers who have scored over 100 Premiership goals before this season?

12 What nationality is Derby County midfielder Aljosa Asanovic?

13 Which six players have won four Championship medals in five years with Manchester United?

14 And who has won five Championship medals in six years?

15 Which Premiership clubs are playing in new stadiums this season?

16 What is the connection between Arsenal manager Arsene Wenger and England manager Glenn Hoddle?

17 Which newly-promoted club is known as 'The Shakers'?

Question 2

18 Which Scottish side plays at Dens Park?

19 Who scored the goals in Chelsea's FA Cup Final success last season?

20 Which Premiership club avoided relegation last season by beating Spurs in their last game?

21 Who was manager of Newcastle United before Kevin Keegan?

22 What was the score in last season's European Cup Final?

23 Which ground is shared by AC Milan and Inter?

24 Who lost the Division One play-off Final at Wembley last May?

25 For which European competition did Newcastle United qualify by finishing second in the Premiership last season?

ANSWERS

25. *Champions' League.*
24. *Sheffield United.*
23. *The San Siro Stadium.*
22. *Borussia 3 - Juventus 1.*
21. *Ossie Ardiles.*
20. *Coventry City.*
19. *Di Matteo and Newton.*
18. *Dundee.*
17. *Bury.*
16. *Wenger was manager of Monaco in France when Hoddle won a French Championship with the club.*
15. *Derby County and Bolton Wanderers.*
14. *Cantona (with Leeds Utd and Manchester Utd.*
13. *Schmeichel, Irwin, Pallister, McClair, Cantona and Giggs.*
12. *Croatian.*
11. *Alan Shearer and Les Ferdinand.*
10. *Paris St Germain.*
9. *They postponed a match at Blackburn without Premiership approval and were fined three points. When the match was finally played, Boro could only draw, dropping another two points.*
8. *Estonia.*
7. *Wimbledon.*
6. *David Beckham was born in London. All others were born in the Manchester area.*
5. *He would be the only manager to win the Championship with three different clubs (after Liverpool and Blackburn).*
4. *Leicester City and Wimbledon.*
3. *Robbie Fowler.*
2. *Parma (Italy).*
1. *It will be the first staged in two countries, Japan and South Korea.*

24

home
internationals

WHEN the draw for the current World Cup qualifying campaign was made, two dates were marked indelibly on the calendar in Riccardo Scimeca's home. Those were when England were scheduled to face Italy.

As a member of the England Under-21 side, the Aston Villa defender was able to look forward to two clashes with the team from his father's homeland as the Young England team embarked on their European Under-21 qualifying games.

Those fixtures might have caused a clash of loyalties in the Scimeca family, who run an Italian restaurant in Birmingham.

"My father, Benito, comes from Sicily and is still very keen on Italian football," says Riccardo. "He does not follow a particular club, but likes to watch all the Italian teams when they are on television.

"When England play against Italy, it is a big occasion in the family, but it it did not cause a problem that I played for the England Under-21 team when the two countries met.

"My father is very proud of me and would have been happy whether I had played for England or Italy. He always wants me to do well, and that applies even when I face his own country.

"He came over here when he was young and although he still has relatives in Italy, whom we visit from time to time, most of his family now live in England.

"I suppose I have had a traditional Italian upbringing in the sense that it is very family orientated. We are all very close. We eat Italian food and, although I was born here and have lived in England all my life, my father often speaks to me in Italian at home. I am not perfectly fluent, but I get by okay.

"However, although it is an Italian trait that sons often follow their father into the family business, I don't think that would have been my course.

"If I hadn't become a professional footballer, I would probably have stayed on at school, then gone to university. What career I would have chosen, however, I do not know.

"Despite my background, I feel more English than Italian, and was very proud when asked to play for England in the Under-21 side."

Scimeca has made a remarkable comeback from a serious injury early in his career to carve out a place in the Villa and the Young England side. His career had hardly begun when it came to an abrupt halt.

"I've been at Villa since leaving school and progressed from being a trainee," he says. "A few years ago, I fractured my fibula and tore the ligaments in my ankle at the same time.

"It kept me out of football for a year. But, though it was a bad injury, I don't think there was ever a serious threat to my chances of coming back.

"It is a fairly common injury nowadays — team-mate Gary Charles missed all of last season with a similar one — and, though it took a long time to get over, there was never a doubt in my own mind that I would make it back."

Scimeca has made up that lost ground, and is grateful for the help he received from Dave Sexton, who was a coach at Villa while Scimeca was battling to make the grade as a youngster.

"Dave had a lot of influence on me while I was coming through the ranks," says Scimeca. "He stuck by me and helped me to develop my skills. He is a very experienced man who has been with a lot of clubs, and it was very important to me to have him around when I was a youngster.

"Now, of course, he is assistant to Peter Taylor, the England Under-21 manager, and is still helping me."

> Despite my background, I feel more English than Italian

SOUTHAMPTON egil **OSTENSTADT**

dropped!

Newcastle's Steve Watson brings Graham Stuart, Everton, down to earth.

h man

STEFFEN IVERSEN'S 12 - month season

By the time the young Norwegian striker joined Tottenham Hotspur in December 1996, his season was already eight months old. It took a super-human effort for him to keep going until the end of the Premiership in May.

He'd dreamed of sunning himself on the warm beaches of the West Indies. Instead, he had to learn all about life in the English Premiership.

"I would have loved to have had a holiday," says Steffen. "The problem was that Tottenham needed me to play immediately.

"So I just had to get on with it. I wasn't complaining because it was a wonderful opportunity for me to come and play in England.

"I've never worried about playing too much football. When I was a young boy growing up in Norway I would play for hours on end with my friends.

"The training is hard at Tottenham but I soon got used to it. Being naturally fit is a big help."

Iversen made a big impression on Spurs' boss Gerry Francis when playing for Norwegian champions, Rosenborg. Over eight months, he watched him many times and, after a while, Francis was joined by several other admiring managers from the Premiership.

Francis was one step ahead of the rest. He invited Steffen and his family over to have a look around White Hart Lane and he even had one of his friends already on the staff.

"Goalkeeper Espen Baardsen was a friend of mine from the Norwegian Under-21 side," says Steffen. "He told me all about the club and that made my decision to come here much easier.

"There's no doubt Espen was a big influence on my decision to join Spurs. It also helped that I could speak Norwegian with him.

"My family and I were very impressed when we first came to Tottenham to look around. I could tell this was a big club who would look after me well.

"Before finally coming to England to sign for Tottenham, I had one last game to play for Rosenborg. That was a Champions League fixture against AC Milan in the famous San Siro Stadium.

"It was quite a night to go out on. We beat the great Italians 2-1 and qualified for the quarter-finals of the Cup.

"Before the match I didn't think we had a chance. But we really went at them and took everybody by surprise.

"The feeling that night is hard to describe. I certainly didn't get much sleep with the excitement of the result and the thought of joining Tottenham the very next day.

"I was up at eight o'clock the following morning to catch a plane to England. Despite Rosenborg's great result, I still wanted to join Tottenham.

"I knew it would be very different playing in England. In Norway I was used to having a lot of space to play in but the tough defenders in the Premier League don't allow that.

"In the Premiership you have to be quick, think quick and be tough. You have to get used to the pace of the game to survive.

"The Norwegians have done very well in England recently. Henning Berg, Stig Bjornebye and Øyvind Leonhardsen have all made a big impression in the Premiership.

"I particularly enjoyed facing Henning when we played against Blackburn. He's one of my country's top defenders so it was great to score a goal against him."

One of the first jobs Iversen had to do when he joined Tottenham was choose what shirt he wanted to wear. With natural confidence, he selected the number 18 — that previously worn by Jurgen Klinsmann.

With his blond hair and eye for goal, comparisons between Steffen and the great German were inevitable. However, he is very much is own man.

"I didn't want to be the second Jurgen Klinsmann. I wanted to be the first Steffen Iversen.

> **I didn't want to be the second Jurgen Klinsmann. I wanted to be the first Steffen Iversen**

"Of course I knew all about what Jurgen had done at Tottenham. My job was to make a similar impression on the fans.

"In Norway I was already used to being compared with another famous footballer — my father Odd, who was a great goalscorer for Rosenborg twenty years ago. I didn't want it happening in England too."

Steffen made a promising start at White Hart Lane. But he had to do without the help of either Teddy Sheringham or Chris Armstrong who were injured during his first few months at the club.

It was a big responsibility for the 21-year-old. Spurs were ravaged by injuries and he was carrying the main goalscoring hopes for the team.

When things started to get a bit difficult for Steffen, Gerry Francis found the perfect way to boost his confidence — he showed him a video of all the great goals he had scored, including a hat-trick for Norway's Under-21's.

It worked a treat. The very next night he went out and scored a stunning hat-trick in the 4-0 win at Sunderland.

That left the Spurs' fans singing just one song "There's only one Steffen Iversen."

"A goal is a goal but after scoring three that night, I made sure I kept the ball," he says. "There's nothing like scoring goals to help your confidence." ●

short
changed!

Everton
have
made a
new man
of CRAIG
SHORT

30

mOTIVATION. PREPARATION. DIET. Three key words which sum up the transformation in Craig Short since he began to establish himself at the heart of the Everton defence.

The former Derby County star made a faltering start to his Goodison Park career following his £2.4 million move from the Baseball Ground.

Since then, he has been a rock in Everton's defence.

He admits that the completion of his settling-in period on Merseyside partly explains the upturn in fortunes, but puts it down mostly to a complete change in his living habits during the days leading up to a match.

That, and former manager Joe Royle's unusual way of psyching him up!

Says Craig, "Since I arrived at Everton, I have been much more aware of the need for proper preparation. As soon as I signed for the club, I realised that it was not so much a physical adjustment I would have to make, but a mental one.

"I'm quite a laid-back person and it takes a lot to get me wound up, but I'm always at my best when I am aggressive and psyched up.

"If I went out on to the pitch feeling too relaxed, and therefore lackadaisical, I would struggle. Maybe that was part of my problem during my first season at Goodison.

"I often need a kick up the backside to get me going and Joe Royle recognised the importance of that. He knew what made me tick.

"For instance, when we played against Sheffield Wednesday at Hillsborough towards the end of the season before last, he was having a laugh and a joke with us in the dressing room ten minutes before kick-off.

"Suddenly, he shouted, 'Come on, lads, get yourselves going!' and, as he did so, turned to me and slapped me across the face.

"He took me completely by surprise, then stepped back and burst out laughing.

"There was nothing malicious in the slap. He was just reminding me that I needed to get motivated and did it in a humorous way. It was his way of telling me what I needed to do myself and it worked. We went out and won 5-2.

"Other previous managers have recognised the need to get me wound up before a match. Neil Warnock, my boss at Scarborough and Notts County, used to shout and bawl at me in the dressing room.

"We had some good players at County, but a lot of the success was down to the way Neil got us going. We were a horrible side to play against. We had great team spirit and worked hard for each other.

"That's what our game is about at Everton. When we have not done well during the past year, it has been on the occasions when we have not been so committed and haven't managed to attain that aggression level."

That commodity has not been lacking in Short during his current run, in which he has given the impression that he would run through a brick wall if necessary.

"That's my game," he goes on. "I am a 6ft 3in defender, and not the type of player who can spray 40-yard passes around.

"During my Scarborough days, Neil Warnock once said to me, 'Short, there are those who carry the bricks and those who lay the bricks. You just make sure you carry them and let others lay them!'

"That was his way of telling me to play to my strengths and let others play to theirs. My physical strength is my main asset, and I need to be a presence on the field. That means being committed.

"Since I came to Everton, our coach, Willie Donachie, has preached much the same message. But he also has a lot of ideas about how to get your mind properly tuned for a match and I have been following many of his guidelines.

"I now have a routine which dictates my activities and my diet, particularly during the 48 hours immediately prior to a game.

"In the lower divisions, and with smaller clubs, you can often get by just on natural ability.

"Now I am playing against the best in the country and virtually my whole way of life has to be geared to competing with them.

"That means I have become a bit selfish at home, especially on Friday evenings and Saturday mornings. I tend to go into a shell and lock myself away from other people.

"Fortunately, my wife, Joanne, understands and helps to create the right atmosphere for me.

"We discourage friends from coming round on Friday evenings, so that I have no distractions. Our young daughter, Beth, goes to bed early, so then we will relax and go to bed around 10 pm.

"I have a full night's sleep and am up fairly early in the morning to go out for a walk with the dog. While I am out, I start to become mentally focussed for the match in the afternoon.

"Willie Donachie's theory is that the first 10 to 20 minutes of a match are the most important, especially for a defender. He tells us that, if you have a sloppy start, it is always difficult to recover.

"By making sure you have the right mental preparation, however, you can avoid that sloppiness and be positive right from the first whistle."

By regulating his diet, Short has also helped himself prepare properly for games.

He goes on, "I've cut out red meat, potatoes and bread, but increased my intake of fresh vegetables and fruit. I also drink a lot of bottled mineral water.

"Previously, my eating patterns were always a bit hit and miss. Sometimes, I would eat the right foods. At other times, I would just let myself go.

"I certainly didn't stock up on pasta for two days before a match, as I do now. I wouldn't say I ate junk food, but often had meals which probably were not the best preparation.

"The important thing is that I now have a set pattern, which I believe has helped me. Cynics probably think the routine which sets my diet and mental preparation is all a bit stupid, but I am convinced it has helped me to become a better player." ●

> **"Now I am playing against the best in the country and virtually my whole way of life has to be geared to competing with them."**

frank talkir

THE WORLD CUP CAN'T COME TOO SOON FOR CHELSEA'S FRANK LEBOEUF!

BRAZIL kick off in Paris, on June l0, 1998, in the biggest World Cup tournament ever seen. World Cup 1998, featuring 32 finalists, will be the climax of a qualifying marathon involving 170 nations, and taking in 639 matches.

37 billion television viewers worldwide are expected to tune in for the month-long Finals.

The French organisers hope to sell 2.5 million match tickets.

Over 9,000 media folk will work to report every facet of the finals to a global television, radio and newspaper audience.

The whole of France has been gearing up for 1998 for the past five years. It will be a festival of football similar to EURO 96 but on double the scale.

Chelsea defender Frank Leboeuf hopes to be there as part of Aime Jacquet's French squad. The Stamford Bridge favourite is determined to take part in his country's moment of glory.

"It is for me very important to be part of the French squad. But it is no certainty," says Leboeuf.

"I don't think playing for Chelsea has hurt my chances. Many of the French side are playing club football outside France.

"Chelsea have given me the opportunity to show what I can do. I have learned a lot, and developed more confidence.

"I was unknown when I joined Chelsea. Nothing much was expected from me because of that.

"But when you go to a different country you have make a big adjustment in your life. Everything is very different.

"You have to win a battle on and off the pitch to succeed and establish a regular place. Winning that battle last year gave me a lot more confidence.

"Last season was very good for me. I enjoyed it very much, and I think French coach Aime Jacquet noticed my performances for Chelsea.

"But there are a lot of good players in France. I have to be at my best for Chelsea this season, to stand a chance of selection.

"One of my best friends is Marcel Desailly, now playing with AC Milan in Italy. But he has really damaged my chances of getting in the team!

"Desailly has dropped back from midfield into central defence for France. He is a great player, and it will make things much tougher for me."

Leboeuf loves playing in England. At first, he wasn't sure about joining Chelsea. Now the Frenchman knows he made the right decision.

"Playing in England is completely different. It's much more enjoyable," he continues.

"The atmosphere in the stadiums is fantastic in England. In France it's very quiet at most grounds.

"I love the fans in England, especially at Chelsea. To hear them sing a song about me is unbelievable.

"In France the people love to speak about football. They quite like to watch football.

"They are supporters of football. Of the game itself.

"In England it's a religion. The fans support a team. They go to see their team play, rather than to see a game of football.

"It makes a totally different atmosphere. The crowds are much bigger. Football is more intense in England. For a player, it's much better.

"For the World Cup I think the stadiums in France will be full. The atmosphere will be okay.

"The facilities will be very good. All the stadiums will be brand new or much improved.

"But I don't think the World Cup will transform the game in France. After

> **I don't think playing for Chelsea has hurt my chances.**

Stade de Paris

g

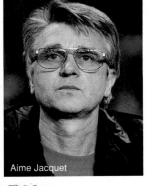

Aime Jacquet

home pitch in the World Cup.

"The ground will be great. It has been enlarged from holding 46,000 to 60,000 all seated for the World Cup.

"Unlike England in 1966 and EURO 96, France will not be playing all our matches in one stadium. It's not good for the public for the players to stay in one place."

In fact, every one of the 32 finalists will play their opening group matches at three different grounds. Each of the ten stadiums will host at least six matches in the tournament.

France, as hosts, will be one of the favourites. In recent years they have produced a string of fine players.

"The players believe France can win the World Cup, but we need the public on our side," says Leboeuf.

"We need to be 12 on the pitch for every match — the 11 players, and the crowd. At EURO 96 I don't think the French public had any belief in us.

"The French press were not on our side. The papers kept telling the people we were a bad team.

"We are stronger now. France has some of the best players in Europe.

"Last season, Monaco defeated Newcastle easily in the UEFA Cup. The two outstanding players were Dumas, in defence, and Benarbia, the attacking midfield player. But neither could get in the French team.

"Benarbia has mission impossible to win a place ahead of Zinedine Zidane, and Youri Djorkaeff.

"In midfield we are very strong. Even without Desailly, we have Didier Deschamps, a good friend of mine, Christian Karembeu, Vincent Guerin, Corentin Martins, and now Patrick Vieira, of Arsenal.

"Djorkaeff, Karembeu, Deschamps and Desailly have all been playing in Italy. Martins and left-back Bixente Lizarazu play in Spain.

"The squad is quite young, but has a lot of experience from around Europe. There is confidence that we can do well in the World Cup.

"It will be hard for me to win a place. But I really hope for it. To play in the World Cup at home would be the highlight of my career." ●

the Finals are over, the grounds will be almost empty again for league matches.

"There will no atmosphere. 20,000 people in a ground holding 60,000, is not good for players.

"That's the way it is. I'm so happy to be playing at Chelsea where the stadium is full every week with fans who are passionate about the team."

The World Cup organising committee in France will spend over 300 million francs on the ten stadiums being used, and much of the money will be provided by the Government or local authorities.

The players believe France can win the World Cup

Around 200 million is going towards the show-piece Stade de Paris, in the St. Denis quarter of the capital.

The brand new stadium will host the opening ceremony and the final, plus seven other matches.

The towering stands, 45 metres and eight floors high, are covered by a roof that weighs 13,000 tons — one and a half times heavier than the Eiffel Tower.

Leboeuf hopes to play on his home ground, the Velodrome in Marseille.

"It's my favourite stadium," he says. "I was born in Marseille. It would be fantastic to play for France on my

Turn the page to see some of France's hopes for 1998

france98

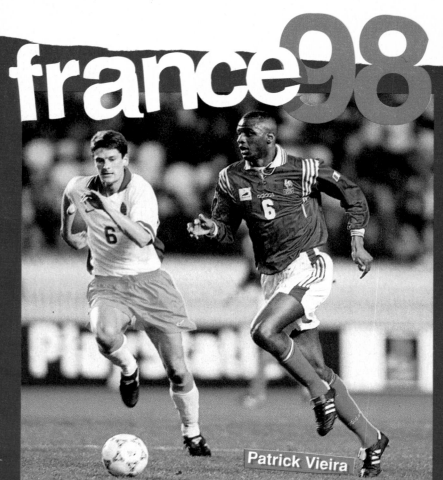

Patrick Vieira

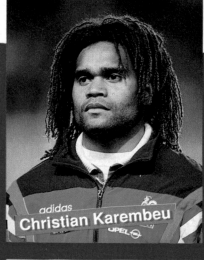

Christian Karembeu

Marcel Desailly

Bixente Lizarazu

Youri Djorkaeff

Zinedine Zidane

Vincent Guerin

Ali Benarbia

CELTIC tosh McKINLAY

LATE

Danish international Per Pedersen arrived at Ewood Park towards the end of last season and was immediately thrust into the first team to help the club avoid relegation from the Premiership.

The £2.5 million striker had no qualms about being thrown in at the deep end, however. The torture of spending three years out of the game through injury has taught him to appreciate every match that comes his way.

As Per explains, the majority of his early career was spent on the treatment table recovering from a catalogue of serious injuries.

He recalls, "I have had three bad knee injuries already in my career. There have been two cruciate ligament injuries to my right knee and the same injury to the left one.

"The first injury came when I was a youngster playing in Denmark against Brondby. Their goalkeeper at the time was Peter Schmeichel, now at Manchester United, and it was in a collision with him that I damaged my knee. It was purely accidental, but it was the beginning of a long injury road for me.

> **I lost three years of my career because of injuries.**

"It was obviously very worrying for me to have so many bad injuries early in my career. I knew that a further knee injury would probably signal the end for me, but I was determined to make a go of my career and fortunately it has picked up for me in recent years.

"To be quite honest, the injuries were all relatively straightforward cruciate ligament tears. Alan Shearer had a similar injury in his early days at Blackburn and recovered from it just like I did. However, he only had one injury to come back from. I had three.

"I lost three years of my career because of my injuries, but the last one was over five years ago and I feel I have done well since. The

starter

PER PEDERSEN is making up for lost time at Blackburn Rovers

injuries aren't something that worry me anymore.

"I don't think there is ever a good time to be injured, but I must admit that it was better for me to have my problems as a young player. I kept my head high when I was out because I was young and I had my whole future in front of me.

"Of course, if you get a cruciate ligament injury when you are older, the hunger and energy to get back may not be the same. What I felt at the time of my injury was that there were a lot of things that I still hadn't experienced. I wanted to get fit because I hadn't achieved anything."

> I wanted to get fit because I hadn't achieved anything.

Since regaining full fitness, Pedersen has achieved most of the things any youngster dreams about. He has earned international recognition with Denmark, scored four times in one game for his country against the USA, and fulfilled a boyhood ambition to play in England.

Per admits, though, that he was beginning to forget about a move abroad. He even made plans to play out his career in Denmark.

He adds, "I was nearly 28 when I signed for Blackburn. Most Scandinavian footballers tend to move abroad earlier than that. I wasn't really considering a move and I actually signed a new four-year contract with my Danish club, Odense.

"I still dreamed of playing in England, but I didn't think about the prospect that often. I was happy to stay in Denmark, but once I was given the opportunity of playing in England, I decided to take it.

"The four goals I scored for Denmark against the USA probably earned me my move. When you score four times in an international people tend to notice and I was soon talking to English clubs.

"When I have been in national squads with English-based players like Mikkel Beck, Claus Thomsen, Peter Schmeichel and Per Frandsen, they all let you know how happy they are in England. They made me quite excited about the prospect of playing in the Premiership.

"The first club to show an interest in me were Bolton Wanderers and I would have signed for them because they were obviously set to be promoted to the Premiership.

"But the move didn't work out and I was very disappointed at the time. I know Bolton's two Danish players, Per Frandsen and Michael Johansen, very well and I was looking forward to linking up with them. Unfortunately it didn't happen, but it turned out to be a good thing.

"Blackburn soon came in with a bid and I was delighted to sign for them. I knew the club from their Championship success in 1995 and they are a bigger, wealthier club than Bolton. My ambition to be successful in England is more likely to be fulfilled at Ewood Park.

"I just hope that nobody expects me to be the new Alan Shearer. I am not annoyed by the comparisons because I know now what Shearer meant to the people of Blackburn, but I want to make my own name." ●

screen

STEVE SCREECH spends hours perfecting his crossing and weeks developing his dribbling skills to world class level.

Sometimes he's up all night working on set-piece moves, corners, his shooting and goalscoring ability.

What's more, Steve also possesses international-class goalkeeping techniques.

But don't go looking for this world-class performer in Glenn Hoddle's England squad. You won't find his name in any of the Premiership line-ups.

Don't even bother scouring the training grounds. For Steve never works up a sweat in practice.

In fact, he produces all his best work sitting down in front of a screen.

Steve is a computer programmer with manufacturers Anco and is responsible for some of the best football games on the market.

These days, virtual reality is the aim when it comes to computer games. Realistic movements, realistic skills, realistic situations. Steve and a team of computer experts produce just that.

Currently they are working on Kick-Off 98, the game that will be launched to coincide with the World Cup Finals in France.

The computer team will make use of the latest state-of-the-art technology to produce new features and make the game more like the real thing.

For the first time, the current game, Kick-Off 97, was produced with the help of top international players, David Seaman, Patrick Vieira and Ian Wright.

The Arsenal stars spent three days, each wired up with more than 20 electronic sensors, going through typical football movements.

Signals from the sensors were fed into a computer, to be reproduced by a three-dimensional 'model' on screen. From this, the programmers were able to capture authentic movement.

"It was hard work for the players," reveals Steve. "It took hours for them to go through a range of different movements.

"It was particularly hard for David Seaman. He had to keep diving this way and that, but very often the impact dislodged the sensors, and he had to do it again.

"Fortunately we had padded mats for him to land on, so it wasn't too bad. David is so easy-going, the toughest part for him was filming the 'frustrated keeper' sequence.

vieira

wright

seaman

"We have a goalkeeper pounding his fists on the ground after conceding a goal. That's completely against David's nature. We had to teach him how to do it!"

Computer experts are now working on ways to improve the capture of authentic movement for future games. More sensors will be used, with information transmitted to the computer model by radio, rather than by wires.

Based on the movements and techniques demonstrated by the Arsenal stars, each player in the game is programmed with a range of options.

The latest development is to give the screen players the same characteristics as the real-life stars.

At Anco, a huge data base of professional players from all over the world, containing personal details, career statistics, appearance and particular skills is building up.

Two experts are constantly collating and updating information on international players. Strengths, weaknesses and style of play are all noted.

By the 1998 World Cup, details of nearly 15,000 players, from countries all over the world, will be logged on computer.

This will enable programmers to reproduce the individual style and characteristics of every squad member of the 32 competing teams at the World Cup Finals. In computer parlance, it's called Artificial Intelligence.

For instance, computer game players selecting to play as 'England', will have

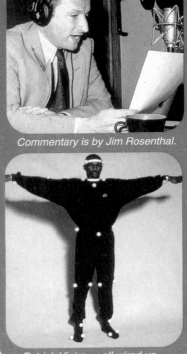

Commentary is by Jim Rosenthal.

Patrick Vieira — all wired up.

a full international squad to choose the team from.

Pick Paul Gascoigne for the team, and you will get a midfield player with great ball control, superb passing ability, and a good free-kick but with limited pace.

Select Alan Shearer, and you get a striker with all the Newcastle star's assets such as pace, strength, determination and great shooting skills.

A defender like Tony Adams is programmed with great strength in the tackle and dominance in the air.

Over 300 international and club teams from around the world are included on the current version. The choice will be even bigger next year.

Computer games are getting better all the time. The graphics improve as machines become more powerful. New features are added in the search for more realism, more professionalism.

But programmers will always leave in one basic feature — the freedom to pick your own team.

You want to play for England in the World Cup Finals? Just do it — thanks to the computer. ●

DERBY COUNTY   darryl POWELL

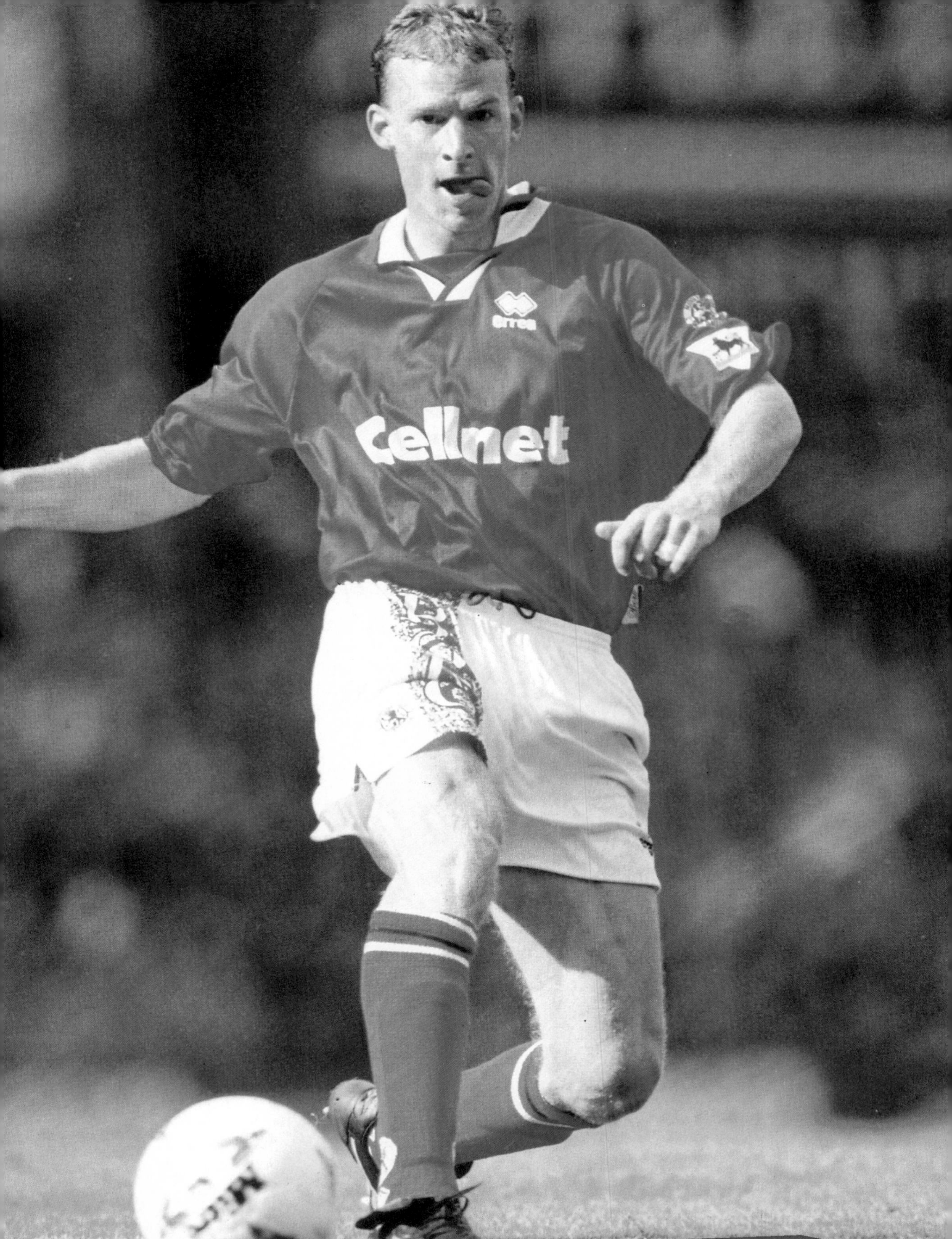

MIDDLESBROUGH

robbie MUSTOE

it's a funny old game

How about this for a super transfer? Italian clubs Polisportira and Sculese decided to stage their own protest against the ever-increasing price of players and agreed that midfielder Guiseppe Murgi could move to Sculese in exchange for a live goat and a slice of ham.

There was an air of friendliness one day when China faced Greece. The teams lined up and stood to attention for the national anthems. The Greeks politely stood for what they thought was the Chinese anthem and the Chinese equally stood to attention thinking that the music was the Greek national anthem. It was actually the new theme music from a toothpaste advert!

Some players in Spain try to bring themselves extra luck by planting a clove of garlic behind the goal. Blackburn Rovers were well ahead of their time — they planted Flowers in their goal several years ago!

It's not often that a referee gets sent off but it happened in Brazil when Luiz Vila Nova sent off Semilde of Urubuetama. As the ref took the player's name, Semilde said something he didn't like. He threw down his notebook and landed a right hook on the player's chin. When Semilde recovered he tried to kick the referee who then went on the attack again. Officials raced on and removed them both, a linesman taking over for the rest of the game.

Everton's Gary Speed is convinced that the house he bought just before leaving Leeds was haunted since there was a lot of unexplained banging about and doors opening. But that is not the only ghostly story connected with soccer. Norwich City fans will tell you about a headless horseman seen riding towards Carrow Road while York City fans believe they have seen a ghostly troop of Roman soldiers walking near Bootham Crescent. And Manchester United fans will tell you they often see a football going through a wall, having been kicked by David Beckham or Eric Cantona!

"... and this one sounds like the lesser-spotted twitter-bird. Listen!"

city slicker

DARREN HUCKERBY
enjoyed being sent to Coventry!

KEVIN KEEGAN made few mistakes in his time as Newcastle United manager, but his decision to disband the club's reserve team two seasons ago could prove to be one of the worst — if Coventry City's Darren Huckerby keeps scoring goals against United.

The 21-year-old striker earned rave reviews at Highfield Road following his £1 million move from Newcastle in November, 1996. He shot to prominence in only his third game for Coventry by scoring in a 2-1 victory against his old club.

Now Huckerby admits that he may never have left Tyneside if the club had not scrapped the second team. As soon as they did, however, he knew it was time to leave.

Darren tells me, "The lack of reserve team football at Newcastle was the reason I decided to leave. I didn't want to sit around doing nothing all season.

"It was very frustrating not to be able to play reserve games. If you weren't in the first team, there was no match to look forward. All we did was train and go home.

"You need reserve games to keep fit and catch the manager's eye, but I didn't have that opportunity.

"I was really disappointed when the side was disbanded. Once that happened, I thought, 'That's it.' I couldn't go on not playing games, so I had to do something. I had a loan spell at Millwall and eventually moved on to Coventry.

"I think I realised last season that I wasn't going to break into the first team on a regular basis. I had played really well after coming as a substitute against Chelsea in the FA Cup and felt I deserved another chance.

"People seemed pleased with my performance, but I didn't keep my place. My situation actually worsened because the club then bought Faustino Asprilla and that dented my chances even further.

"I was disappointed when Kevin Keegan signed Tino. You can't deny that he is a very talented player, but I just wish that Kevin had looked a bit closer to home. I felt that I could have done a job.

"I wasn't bothered when Alan Shearer signed for Newcastle because the club had to buy him. He is the best striker in Europe and any club with the money would have bought him.

"Kevin was all right with me. He obviously had a lot on his plate, but when he had a bit of time he would discuss things with me and keep me involved.

"I had just over 12 months at the club after moving from Lincoln and it was a good experience. However, it would have been nice to have played a few more games. I only made two appearances, both as a sub.

"Maybe the situation at Newcastle wasn't ideal for a young lad like me to have a run in the team. We were going for the Championship and Kevin was under a lot of pressure to do well.

> I felt that I could have done a job for Newcastle

"I can't grumble about my time there, though. It earned me my move to Coventry and I am very happy here.

"I'm very thankful that Ron Atkinson and Gordon Strachan had enough faith in me to bring me to Coventry. I always felt I could score goals at this level and they have given me the chance to prove it.

"Scoring against Newcastle was a nice moment. I wanted to show their fans what I could do because they saw so little of me. I wanted to prove I was a good player and leave them thinking about what I could have done for them. I hope they liked what they saw."

43

back in the big

Leeds United's **NIGEL MARTYN** wants a permanent place in the England scene!

44

time!

FORMER Crystal Palace keeper Nigel Martyn knew that a move to Leeds United would present him with a golden opportunity to get his career moving again.

Back in the summer of 1993, Martyn was competing with David Seaman, Chris Woods and Tim Flowers for a permanent England shirt.

But, by the time Nigel left Selhurst Park in the summer of 1996, he had seen himself drift away from the international scene — despite assurances to the contrary from a former England manager.

It was a time of acute frustration for the 31-year-old as teammates left Selhurst Park for big-time pastures new.

He was desperate to join them, but found his way blocked by factors beyond his control.

Nigel's impressive form and 20 clean sheets in his first full season at Elland Road meant England coach Glenn Hoddle could no longer ignore him, and now he is back as a regular squad member he wants to make up for lost time.

Explains Nigel, "Despite being relegated with Palace, I was picked by Graham Taylor to go on England's 1993 tour of the United States. It was supposed to be a dry run for the next year's World Cup.

"At the time, the Number 1 shirt was up for grabs. It seemed to be an open contest between Chris Woods, Tim Flowers, David Seaman and myself.

"I was picked to play against Germany in Detroit and, although we lost 2-1, I felt I acquitted myself well.

> I'd dropped out of the England picture and into the First Division — without doing anything wrong — and there wasn't a thing I could do about it.

"I was really concerned about how relegation would affect my England prospects and went to see Mr. Taylor about it.

"He assured me that it would not be a problem as long as I continued to perform well. I suppose he was trying to put my mind at rest.

"His words didn't have any bearing on my staying at Palace because I wanted to help the club get back to the Premiership.

"However, it seems that dropping out of the top league did severely affect my chances of an England place.

"I don't bear him any grudges, though, because, although I remained hopeful, it was always going to be hard for an England manager to justify picking a First Division keeper.

"Throughout that season, I played well and Palace got promotion straight back.

"Again we struggled to stay in the Premiership and, despite being picked for an England 'B' game, it was never easy to impress the new England manager, Terry Venables, when Palace were constantly being beaten. All people saw were the goals going past me.

"We were eventually relegated and a lot of players decided they wanted to leave. Gareth Southgate went to Aston Villa, Chris Coleman joined Blackburn and Richard Shaw and John Salako moved to Coventry.

"I was desperate to join them and asked to go on to the transfer list. Nobody came in for me.

"I had hoped that, as an English keeper, clubs struggling with the then European restrictions would be interested. That wasn't the case.

"All the Premiership clubs seemed to have a settled keeper. There wasn't any movement.

"Teams can tinker with their formation to accomodate a new outfield player. You can't do that

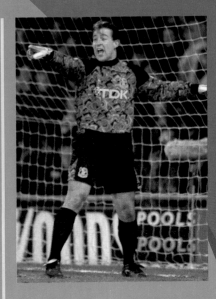

with a goalkeeper.

"Of course that was extremely frustrating. I'd dropped out of the England picture and into the First Division — without doing anything wrong — and there wasn't a thing I could do about it.

"After a while, I decided to sign a new contract with Palace.

"That wasn't down to any lack of ambition. My kid was about to start school and I needed to be settled.

"I still wanted to get back to the top and was absolutely delighted when Leeds paid £2.2 million for me.

"Although I was 30 when I signed for Leeds, I knew that I still had plenty of time to get my England place back.

"The other lads who left Palace had to do so because, as they were into their mid-twenties, they had to get their careers going.

"Keepers only begin to peak in their early thirties and so the time I spent at Palace has not cost me anything.

"I was delighted when Glen Hoddle named me in his squad for the friendly against Mexico last spring. However, much of the credit must go to the Leeds defenders, for although I kept a number of clean sheets I had very little to do.

"I didn't keep count of the number of blanks, I just try to achieve one in every game. Nevertheless, I am as keen as anybody for international recognition and I always knew that if I was given another chance I would do myself justice." ●

sspecial

I magine a team including Alessandro del Piero, Matthias Sammer, David Beckham, Paul Ince, Marcel Desailly, Paul Gascoigne and Zinedine Zidane. Then imagine this team playing their doubles — with both sides coached by the legendary Franz Beckenbauer!

This is the fantasy created by ADIDAS for their Predator Traxion boot commercial, "The Difference".

The beginning of the commercial shows a team of superstars being scanned and cloned. Then the two sets of players take to the field and, with the magic of special effects, actually play against themselves, the best v. the best. However, one team is wearing the Traxion boots, and they win — with a spectacular goal scored by del Piero. This confirms the difference a soccer boot can make!

Commercials for sports equipment are becoming more and more spectacular. Here is some of the stunning photography used in this amazing advertisement.

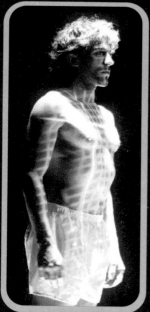

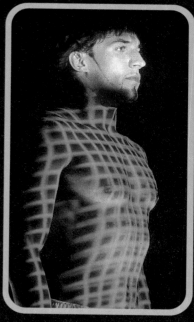

effectsts

The News

48

changed the life of Portsmouth's
LEE BRADBURY

LEE BRADBURY went for a look around Fratton Park one day during the summer of 1995 and by the time he had finished, he was on the way to swapping life in the Army for a career with Portsmouth!

The Isle of Wight-born striker followed in the footsteps of former Pompey star Guy Whittingham by trading a career in the military for a chance in professional football.

Bradbury would love to emulate Whittingham and carve out a career in the top flight. Lee is hoping that his tough Army grounding will give him a head start in the 'easier' environment of the football world.

His immediate target is to build on the progress he made during Pompey's FA Cup run last season.

Says Lee, "I signed up for the Army as a boy soldier when I was 15 and had four-and-half very enjoyable years in the services. I wasn't looking to get out when Pompey offered me a chance, but things just developed that way.

"As a kid, my two aims in life were to be a soldier and footballer. I had a few trials when I was younger, but nothing came of them. In one trial game for Southampton, I injured my knee and that was that.

"When I realised that I might not find a club, I signed up for the Army because they told me that if I was a good footballer, they would exploit my talent and make sure I had every opportunity to play football all over the world.

"It worked out really well because I played plenty of football for both the Army and the Combined Services and went to places as far afield as Hong Kong. I was in the side that won the Infantry Cup in Germany and enjoyed some good times.

"Having left the Army for Portsmouth, people obviously ask if it had anything to do with Guy Whittingham making the same move. It was by pure coincidence that I ended up at Pompey as well.

"The Army team that I was playing for was in Portsmouth and we went to Fratton Park to have a look around the ground. However, one of my coaches told Pompey manager Terry Fenwick that he might want to have a look at me and the club offered me a trial.

"I went to Scotland with the team, came on as a substitute three times and scored three goals. They offered me a contract and I signed. I was a private at the time and was about to take my corporal's course, but I felt the time was right to try something else.

"I had just spent two years serving in Northern Ireland. Looking back, I enjoyed it, but it wasn't easy at first. I served in Omagh and Armagh and I had just turned 18 when I went there.

"That is the youngest you can be to patrol the streets and I was out there doing the job a soldier in Ireland has to do. I was a bit wary in the early days about what I was doing, but I did enjoy it and it felt good to do something that was worthwhile.

> **The goals have come along quite regularly. The hard bit and the real test is sustaining it.**

"The things I learned about fitness and discipline will hopefully stand in my favour. The Army puts you on the right track and gives you a sense of how things are. It certainly didn't do me any harm.

"Football people believe that if you haven't served a footballing apprenticeship, you haven't had it hard. The lads at Pompey are always on about their apprenticeships, but I can't take them seriously.

"I tell them that they have had no apprenticeship like mine! For a whole year, I was up at six every morning doing intensive training and long runs. I enjoyed it, though. The closest your average footballer gets to that is a couple of weeks during pre-season training.

"I have been happy with the way things have gone for me since I left the Army. The goals have come along quite regularly, but that's the easy part. The hard bit and the real test is sustaining it.

"That is my target and hopefully, I can progress enough to emulate Guy Whittingham. Our similar backgrounds will lead to obvious comparisons, but I don't mind at all.

"Guy has made it into the Premiership and built a good reputation for himself. He has reached the top of his profession and I'd be delighted if I have a career like he has had so far."

Guy Whittingham in scoring mood for Portsmouth

of

There's a touch of tartan to Wimbledon's
NEIL SULLIVAN!

WHO will ever forget David Beckham's amazing 'goal of the century' on the opening day of last season? Not Neil Sullivan, that's for sure.

The Wimbledon keeper was the unwitting victim of Beckham's outrageous strike from within his own half. For a while it left Sullivan at the wrong end of many cruel jokes.

Not for long. Neil fought back brilliantly with a series of stunning displays during a season in which Wimbledon were gunning for major honours.

Now he can look back on it as the goal that launched an international career.

"The Beckham goal made everybody talk about me," says Neil. "I didn't want that sort of publicity, but it just made me determined to prove the critics wrong.

"For a while, it didn't get any better. In the very next game, I was beaten by another long-range effort by Newcastle's David Batty. I just kept looking forward to the next game.

"It was one of those moments in your career when things could go either way. I might have gone into my shell and crumbled.

"The alternative was just to get on with it. That's exactly what I set out to do — with the help of Wimbledon's Crazy Gang.

"The Wimbledon lads are great to be around. They quickly made

LONDON SCO

50

me forget about the goal.

"I don't really think I deserved all the stick I took from the critics. That's just the way it goes in football — we goalkeepers always get the blame.

"David Seaman was my inspiration to help me put 'that' goal right behind me. He's my big hero among all the top goalkeepers in the Premiership.

"Over the last few years there's no doubt in my mind that he's been the number one. But like any keeper, he's had his moments to forget.

"The most notable was Nayim's famous goal against David in the European Cup-Winners' Cup Final. It was very similar to David Beckham's effort.

"What's important after that sort of experience is showing the character to fight back. That's exactly what David did and by Euro '96 he was proving to be one of the world's best."

By the middle of last season, Neil had established his credentials as a potential international 'keeper. A Scottish grandfather gave him a qualification for the Scots.

International boss Craig Brown, alerted by Press reports of Sullivan's availability and form for Wimbledon, checked him out.

The Scotland manager rewarded Neil with his first international call-up for the World Cup qualifier against Estonia, in Monaco.

Sullivan didn't have a very easy time trying to establish himself as Wimbledon's number one. Breaking both legs certainly didn't help.

"When I first broke into the team a few years back, I broke my left leg," says Neil. "That meant a long haul before I was back in first-team

Sullivan and Jim Leighton — both wanting to be Scotland's number one.

contention.

"Then, when I finally put myself back into the reckoning, I broke my other leg in the last game of the season.

"It was just one of those things. Everybody gets injuries and you just have to get your head down and work your way back again.

"It wasn't until season 1995-96 that I finally managed to establish myself properly in the Wimbledon first team. It had been a long wait, but it was worth it in the end.

"Last season was when people finally started to take Wimbledon seriously as a football club. It was great to be part of things when that started to happen.

"We were no longer the poor relations. Our success was no fluke and it was great to be there when it all started happening.

"After years of players being ignored, some of the lads were finally getting recognition from their respective countries. Wimbledon

Nobody jokes about Scottish goalkeepers these days. Andy Goram and Jim Leighton have turned that image on its head.

had become an international club.

"People even started talking about me playing at international level — for Scotland. That started me thinking.

"I was born in England but my grandfather was from Glasgow, so I knew that qualified me to play for Scotland. It was just a matter of getting Craig Brown interested.

"Nobody jokes about Scottish goalkeepers these days. Andy Goram and Jim Leighton have turned that image on its head.

"Both have been tremendous servants for Scotland. If there is a chance soon to replace them, then I want to be the man.

"I'm still learning my trade as a keeper. There's still room for improvement in my game.

"We've grown up as a defence together over the last few years. The lads in front of me know all about my game, and I know them very well too.

"Goalkeepers have always been a very important part of the Wimbledon success story. Dave Beasant and Hans Segers both played major roles in the history of the club and now I want to do the same." ●

Beckham scoring THAT goal!

IT'S EVERY footballer's dream to represent his country and I'm no different. But, unlike so many other players up and down the land, I had the chance to live out my dream.

And, I can honestly say, it was the proudest THREE SECONDS of my life!

That was how long my first start for Scotland, in the unlikely setting of the Estonian capital of Tallinn, lasted.

So, even if I never have a chance to pull on the Dark Blue again, at least I can say I took part in one of the most famous internationals EVER!

A prolific goalscoring run for Aberdeen had put me on top of the Scottish goalscoring charts and earned me a place in the national squad for our crucial World Cup qualifiers against the Baltic nations, Latvia and Estonia.

Although the papers had been full of speculation that I would be called up by Craig Brown, I was still stunned when Aberdeen boss Roy Aitken gave me the news.

With the likes of Ally McCoist, John McGinlay, Duncan Ferguson, John Spencer and Gordon Durie all competing for places, you have to be at the top of your game to make it into the squad.

The first thing I did was thank Dean Windass, my

second

Blink and you might have missed

strike partner at Pittodrie.

Deano has been absolutely brilliant since being signed from Hull City and I have him to thank for a lot of my goals.

He's the best strike partner I've ever had, and it is no coincidence that his arrival sparked the best goalscoring form of my career — and my international call-up.

I'd grabbed 14 goals in only 12 outings for Aberdeen, including a couple of hat-tricks, and it was that spree which earned me a place on the bench for our opening Baltic encounter against Latvia.

We made the perfect start when Monaco's John Collins fired in a marvellous shot to give us an early lead.

Another cracking strike, this time from Hibs' Darren Jackson, clinched the points late on and, in between those two classy counters, I'd replaced John Spencer to get my first taste of international

football.

I suppose it would have been a dream start to have netted against Latvia but I wasn't too disappointed.

After all, there was still the Estonia match to come — or so I thought!

Having secured a vital victory in what looked, on paper, to be the trickier of the two ties, the lads were full of confidence as we arrived in Estonia.

And, on a personal level, I was determined to grab a goal if I was given the nod from boss Craig Brown.

I hoped that I'd done enough in my brief appearance against Latvia to warrant a starting berth.

Thankfully, Craig seemed to agree because, when the team was announced on matchday, I was in there at number seven.

That was when things started to get a little bizarre!

We'd heard some strange rumours the evening before suggesting something was up in the Estonian camp but I don't think anyone really took them too seriously.

But, the next morning, we heard that the kick-off time had been shifted because the Estonian

floodlighting wasn't up to scratch.

That didn't affect our preparation too much. We just had a light training session in the morning and made sure we arrived at the Stadium in plenty of time.

The Tartan Army had also managed to be there in time for the revised kick-off and they gave us their usual vocal support!

In fact, the only thing missing was another side for us to play!

But, as the time ticked by towards kick-off, and there was still no sign of the Estonians, Craig Brown was doing his best

to keep us focused.

He kept saying that we shouldn't relax because, for all we knew, the Estonians might arrive at the last moment.

We prepared as normal, listened to Craig's team-talk and trooped out on to the park.

But, with only minutes now left to kick-off time, I knew in my heart that the opposition were not going to turn up.

There wasn't a single home supporter in the ground, so they obviously knew something we didn't!

The referee told our captain Gary McAllister that he was going to abandon the game as soon as we kicked off.

Even so, I made sure I took the kick-off, just in case I got the chance to shoot into an open goal!

After all, goals in international football really don't come any easier!

Unfortunately, the ref spoiled my cunning plan and abandoned the match before I could have a shot.

I'll never forget the support from the Tartan Army!

They were all singing "There's only one team in Tallinn" and who could argue with them!

Sadly for us, when the game was eventually played, we produced a pretty poor performance and could only manage a 0-0 draw.

Just as disappointing for me was the fact that I'd dropped out of the international scene after a barren spell at club level.

But I'm still confident that we'll qualify for France in 1998 and hopefully I'll manage to do well enough to stake a claim for a World Cup berth.

Even if I don't make it, at least I'll still be able to claim I played in the 'The game that never was!' ●

sOut!

it but Aberdeen's BILLY DODDS didn't!

emile **HESKEY**

BORUSSIA DORTMUND — stefan **REUTER**

Mike McDowell was watching —

Just before the end —

OOOOOH! THAT WAS ALMOST NUMBER TWO FOR CITY!

BUT THEY'VE GOT A CORNER...

ALAN BRADLEY'S GOOD... BUT HE'LL NEVER REPLACE BRYAN BROWNING!

ALAN BRADLEY! WHAT A HEADER! TWO-NIL!

A COUPLE OF GREAT GOALS, ALAN. IF I WAS YOU, I RECKON I'D FORGET ABOUT PLAYING FOR ENGLAND!

HAVEN'T YOU GOT SCOTTISH AND WELSH GRANDPARENTS? YOU COULD PLAY FOR EITHER OF THOSE COUNTRIES.

THAT'S TRUE. BUT MY AMBITION HAS ALWAYS BEEN TO PLAY FOR THE COUNTRY OF MY BIRTH... AND I STILL WANT TO!

After every home game, Alan visited his widowed Mother —

HI, MUM... HOW'S IT GOING?

COME IN... YOU'RE JUST IN TIME TO SEE YOURSELF ON TV!

THEY'RE SHOWING THE BEST GOALS OF THE DAY!

I WAS QUITE PLEASED WITH THAT ONE!

DESPITE GOALS LIKE THESE, THERE'S NO SIGN THAT ENGLAND COACH MIKE McDOWELL IS CONSIDERING GIVING ALAN BRADLEY A PLACE IN THE ENGLAND SIDE.

I WAS TALKING TO SOME OF THE LADS TODAY. THEY RECKONED I SHOULD USE MY GRANDPARENTS' QUALIFICATIONS TO PLAY FOR SCOTLAND OR WALES. BUT I TOLD THEM I WANTED TO PLAY FOR THE COUNTRY I WAS BORN IN!

THEN YOU SHOULD BE PLAYING FOR SPAIN! THAT'S WHERE YOU WERE BORN!

WHAT?

WHEN YOUR FATHER WAS IN THE DIPLOMATIC CORPS, WE WERE BASED IN MADRID. YOU WERE BORN THERE. WE FLEW BACK TO ENGLAND WHEN YOU WERE A FEW DAYS OLD!

A few days later, at the Spanish Embassy —

IT IS QUITE TRUE, SENOR BRADLEY. OUR RECORDS SHOW YOUR PLACE OF BIRTH AS MADRID.

AND I ALWAYS THOUGHT I WAS BORN IN ENGLAND!

A week after Alan's amazing discovery, there was an international match between Spain and Belgium —

BENITO BELLITROS! OVER THE BAR!

IT WOULD HAVE BEEN EASIER TO SCORE!

Manager Emilio Sanchez despaired!

SINCE WE LOST MANUEL ZAPPATTA WITH SERIOUS INJURY, WE CANNOT FIND ANYONE TO SCORE GOALS FOR US!

MAYBE THERE IS A SOLUTION, EMILIO! I HAVE HAD A TIP-OFF FROM A FRIEND WHO WORKS IN THE SPANISH EMBASSY IN LONDON . . .

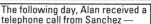

The following day, Alan received a telephone call from Sanchez —

THAT IS CORRECT, ALAN . . . I WANT YOU TO PLAY FOR SPAIN, THE PLACE WHERE YOU WERE BORN. YOUR COUNTRY NEEDS YOU!

WELL, SEEING MY CHANCES OF PLAYING FOR ENGLAND AREN'T TOO GOOD . . .

All the necessary paperwork was completed, and Alan was introduced to his new team-mates before their next match —

THIS IS JULIO ENRICHO. YOU WILL BE PLAYING ALONGSIDE HIM IN NEXT WEEK'S INTERNATIONAL.

BETWEEN US WE SCORE MANY GOALS. RIGHT, ALAN?

As fate would have it, Spain's next match was a friendly at Wembley —

WHEN I WALKED OUT TO PLAY AN INTERNATIONAL AT WEMBLEY, I ALWAYS THOUGHT I'D BE WEARING AN ENGLAND SHIRT!

BUT NOW I'M IN THE COLOURS OF SPAIN . . . AND I'VE GOT TO DO MY BEST FOR THEM!

I'VE HIT THE POST! I THOUGHT THAT WAS IN!

BUT I CAN GET TO THE REBOUND!

IT'S THERE! ONE-NIL TO SPAIN!

CHELSEA **gianfranco** ZOLA

SPURS darren **ANDERTON**

dann

A move to Barnsley was a st

Danny Wilson

WHILE Fabrizio Ravanelli and Juninho grabbed the headlines with their exploits at the Riverside Stadium last season, their predecessors at Middlesbrough quietly got on with some praiseworthy work of their own.

Once Barnsley manager Danny Wilson parted with £250,000 and teamed up John Hendrie with his old Boro strike partner Paul Wilkinson at the beginning of October 1996, his team never looked back.

As Bryan Robson's expensively-assembled side enjoyed two long cup runs but slid down the Premiership table, Hendrie's goals fired the unfashionable South Yorkshire side to an unexpected promotion to the top division for the first time in their 111-year history.

The move to Barnsley is one that Hendrie will never regret — even though he believes that it cost him two cup final appearances and a lot of money!

Says John, "I have to be honest and say that I didn't envisage we'd be in this situation when I arrived at Oakwell. It has worked out unbelievably well.

"When I arrived, Danny Wilson told me that things could happen here. Paul Wilkinson said the same. Yet, it is still better than I thought.

"I'm in the twilight of my career and there is no doubt that leaving Middlesbrough for Barnsley was a step down. Now it looks like a step back to go forward again.

"I could have stayed at Boro until my contract ran out at the end of last season and then taken it from there. The manager, Bryan Robson, left it up to me.

"Barnsley, though, really appealed because it allowed me to stay in Yorkshire, my home for the

> ## I didn't see any disgrace in losing my place to world-class talents like Ravanelli and Juninho.

last 12 years. If I'd waited until the summer to sort something out, who knows where I'd have ended up?

"Although football reasons weren't the main priority for the move, I didn't want to see out my days in the comfort zone. Barnsley's success means I'm still testing myself.

"I could have stayed at Boro and sat on the bench. I'd been involved in every game, either as a sub or playing, before I moved and there is no reason to suggest that would have changed.

"That would have meant trips to Wembley for the Coca-Cola and FA Cup Finals and some medals. That would have been nice.

"In fact, there were players who played in the cup finals, like Craig Hignett and Clayton Blackmore, who I was ahead of in the pecking order. Maybe I would have even played at Wembley.

"I definitely missed out on the bonuses the Boro lads got for reaching two finals!

"I've no regrets, though, and I didn't see any disgrace in losing my place to world-class talents like Ravanelli and Juninho. I'd like to think, though, I could have done as good a job as someone like Mikkel Beck.

"Any disappointments I may have felt at missing out with Middlesbrough were more than made up for by Barnsley's promotion. It's great to see the excitement and anticipation around the place.

"I've won promotion to the top division before at Leeds and at Middlesbrough but this ranks as the greatest achievement of the lot. To be a Premiership side on Barnsley's resources is something else." ●

y'sBOY

the right direction for JOHN HENDRIE — eventually!

Alan Shearer's goal-scoring record speaks for itself. Before his £15 million transfer to Newcastle last August, he had scored over one hundred goals for Blackburn Rovers. Then, in his first season with the Magpies, he hit the target twenty seven times despite being out for part of the season through injury.

Alan's goals come in all forms — close in or far out... shot or header.

Such natural goal-scoring makes him one of the world's top strikers.

We asked Alan to select ten of his best — and most memorable — goals...

best

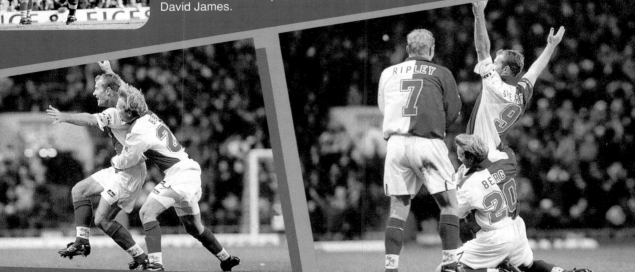

goal ① April, 1988. First Division. What a way to start my career as a professional footballer! My full debut for Southampton against Arsenal at The Dell and I score a hat-trick in a 4-2 victory.

Although it was a while before I established myself in the first-team, it's a day I will certainly never forget.

goal ② February, 1992. My first game for my country and my first goal. It was a dream start to my international career.

France came to Wembley on the back of a long unbeaten run, but my goal helped England to a 2-0 victory. It was quite a simple goal, a turn and shot from six yards, but it meant a lot.

goal ③ August, 1992. Premiership. I had just signed for Blackburn in a British record transfer from Southampton. It was my debut for Rovers and the club's first game in the top flight for 26 years so it was a big day.

I scored twice in a 3-3 draw with Crystal Palace, but my first goal sticks out. From 25 yards, I curled the ball past Nigel Martyn and into the top corner.

goal ④ August, 1993. Premiership. My first goal after recovering from my cruciate ligament injury came against Newcastle at St James' Park.

I had been out for nine months and was desperate to play again. Blackburn manager Kenny Dalglish wanted to ease me back in, though, and restricted me to substitute appearances.

I came off the bench at Newcastle and scored. I sprinted onto a through ball and poked the ball past Pavel Srnicek in front of the Gallowgate End.

goal ⑤ May, 1995. Premiership. This goal was one of the most important of my career. Blackburn had to beat Newcastle to stay on course for the Championship, but it was a tense game.

My goal was enough in a 1-0 win, but much of the credit goes to Graeme Le Saux. His run to the by-line and far-post cross meant I had to score. I climbed above John Beresford and headed into the net.

As we lost our next game against Liverpool, the header against Newcastle effectively clinched the Championship.

goal ⑥ May, 1995. Premiership. Although we lost to Liverpool, we still managed to pip Manchester United to the Championship.

The goal I scored at Anfield didn't win us any points, but it calmed the nerves and upped the pressure on United. Stuart Ripley's cross was inch-perfect and I slotted the ball past David James.

goal ⑦ December, 1995. Premiership. Personal milestones don't matter to me, but it was nice to become the first player to score 100 goals in the Premiership.

Tottenham were the opposition at Ewood Park and I scored a goal past Ian Walker from outside the penalty area to break the 100 barrier.

goal 8 **August, 1996. Premiership**. My first game at St James' Park after signing for Newcastle and the whole crowd was willing me to score my first goal for the club.

Fortunately, I managed to oblige with a free-kick. From about 20 yards, I curled the ball around the Wimbledon wall and into the top corner. I had always dreamed of scoring in a black-and-white shirt and it came true that night.

goal 9 **June, 1996. Euro '96.** I had gone 13 games without a goal for England and many people were questioning where the next one would come from. It came at the best possible time, in our opening Euro '96 game against Switzerland.

I sprung the off-side trap and fired past the Swiss goalkeeper from a narrow angle.

goal 10 **October, 1996. World Cup Qualifier.** Poland gave us a tough game at Wembley and went ahead, but fortunately we pulled the game around. The two goals I scored took me into the all-time top 20 leading goalscorers for England.

The second goal went in from 25 yards and Les Ferdinand had to take evasive action to get out of the way!

REAL MADRID roberto CARLOS

lee BOWYER

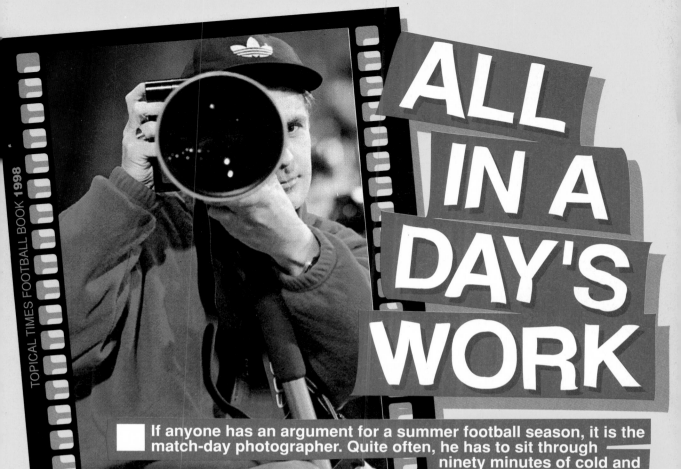

TOPICAL TIMES FOOTBALL BOOK 1998

ALL IN A DAY'S WORK

If anyone has an argument for a summer football season, it is the match-day photographer. Quite often, he has to sit through ninety minutes of cold and rain to bring you the best of the day's action. Luckily, the weather was perfect when the "Topical Times" spent a day with top snapper Phil Cole!

8.30 am

First thing, a chat with colleague Tony Graham to discuss which match Phil will be taking in that day.

9.30 am

Down to the film store. Phil goes through an average of six films every game. For the camera enthusiasts among you, Phil uses 400 Fuji RDP and 800 Fuji negative film.

10.00 am

All set for the long drive. Phil clocks up around 1,000 miles a week!

12.30 pm

On arrival at the ground, Phil checks his equipment. He carries around £10,000 worth of cameras and accessories.

1.00 pm

Today it's Wimbledon v Aston Villa, and Selhurst Park has been notified of Phil's arrival.

2.30 pm

The Villa players warm up before the match — and so does Phil!

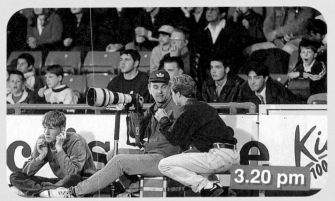

3.20 pm

■ Phil has a Film Editor/Technician on hand to take away any films that are finished and start the processing.

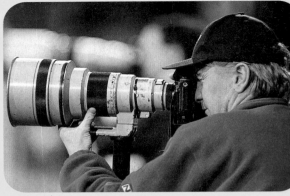

■ Phil gets a close-up of the action.

■ Packing up. Now there's only one thing left to do . . .

4.45 pm

TOPICAL TIMES FOOTBALL BOOK **1998**

➤ PIC 1

5.00 pm

■ . . . and that's to wire his pictures direct from the ground to his office.

9.00 pm

■ Back at H.Q. Phil checks his pictures with John Paul Temple, Picture Desk Editor.

■ Next day and Phil admires his work in the morning papers.

FUJI 400 RDP

■ Wimbledon v Aston Villa — as seen through Phil's lens.

➤ PIC 1

■ A quick break before Phil tackles his next assignment. A keen golf fan, Phil would love it to be the Augusta Masters — but is more likely to be Aldershot versus Mansfield!

PIC 1

■ We asked Phil to pick his favourite photograph. This was taken at an Arsenal v Crystal Palace match in August 1994.

FUJI 400 RDP

PIC 1

■ Our thanks to Lee Martin and the "Allsport" staff for their help in making this feature.

71

The MIDFIELD MAGICIAN
The story of GLENN HODDLE

Glenn Hoddle, the cultured midfield general whose displays for Spurs and Monaco in the 1980s ranked him among the best in the world. After a short managerial career with Swindon Town and Chelsea, he became the England coach after Euro'96.

Glenn was born on 27th October, 1957, in Hayes, Middlesex. Right from an early age, Glenn's father encouraged him to play football.

Glenn's first organised team was Potter Street Rangers. Glenn was only 10 and the rest of the lads were a lot older but his talent shone through.

Glenn went to Burnt Mill School, Harlow. As well as being a star of the school side, he turned out for Essex Under-15s.

Glenn was also a fine rugby player. He played fly-half for the West Essex rugby select.

Glenn had always been an avid ~~s~~purs fan. When he had time, he ~~us~~ed to go to White Hart Lane to ~~se~~e them play. Martin Chivers was ~~on~~e of his favourite players.

Glenn was spotted by Spurs playing Sunday League soccer. In April, 1974, he signed as an apprentice, becoming a full professional in 1975.

In 1982, Glenn became the first player to score in both a Wembley Cup Final and the subsequent replay. His penalty against QPR gave Spurs the Cup for the second successive year.

In 1987, Hoddle joined Monaco, and the next year he was the first Englishman to be part of a French championship-winning side.

In 1993, Hoddle, in the role of player-manager, led Swindon Town into the top division for the first time in the Wiltshire club's history. The following season, he took over as player-manager of Chelsea, taking the Stamford Bridge club to the FA Cup Final. There they lost 4-0 to Manchester United.

★★★★★★★★★★★★★
In May, 1996, at the age of 38, Hoddle took over the England job from Terry Venables. Can he surpass the efforts of his immediate predecessors and lead England to World Cup glory in June?
★★★★★★★★★★★★★

roy KEANE

jorg **ALBERTZ**

Mark Crossley — Nottingham Forest's honorary Welshman!

mARK CROSSLEY'S first cap for Wales in their friendly with the Republic of Ireland last season was as much a reward for perseverance as for his performances for Nottingham Forest.

It was, after all, his third attempt at kick-starting an international career!

Despairing of his chances of getting full recognition from the country of his birth, the Barnsley-born holder of three England U-21 caps decided he could wait no longer for the then national coach, Terry Venables, to give him a call.

He was in the best form of his life and felt he warranted a game at the very highest level.

Most players feel the same at some point in their careers but are ultimately left frustrated. Continually overlooked, they are left to reflect on what might have been.

Crossley, though, had other irons in the fire.

Turning to genealogy — the study of family trees — Crossley unearthed some useful relatives. He has both Welsh and Scottish grandparents — enough of a family link to qualify for an international career with either country.

There was still one hitch to overcome, however.

At the time that his thoughts turned to such matters, Forest were embarking on a UEFA Cup run.

With the restrictive three-foreigners rule still in force, the last thing his club wanted was for Crossley to declare himself

third time

> **With the right kind of Welsh and Scottish background, I knew I had a chance of playing international football.**

available to Wales or Scotland. That would have made him a foreign player and, with Forest already having three non-English players on the books, it could have put his place in jeopardy.

Mercifully for the 28-year-old, the 'foreigner' rule was outlawed and he could finally contemplate a career in an international shirt.

He explains, "I had a good season in 1994 when Forest won promotion back to the Premiership and continued that good form in to the next year when we finished third in the League and qualified for Europe.

"I'd shown I was a good keeper before then — but only in patches. Like most young players, I was inconsistent and made the occasional mistake.

"Outfield players often get away with their slips. Goalkeepers aren't so fortunate and some of mine led to goals. I was not what you would call a crowd favourite.

"I knew I had to do something or my career was heading only one way — down. With that knowledge, I worked harder than ever on my game and made myself into a better, more consistent player.

"By the time Forest went into Europe, I believed I was playing as well as any keeper in the country. My then manager, Frank Clark, was of the same mind and pushed me for England recognition.

"His call fell on deaf ears, though. I don't think that playing for Nottingham Forest was doing me any favours.

"For whatever reason, the club does not get much media coverage. Despite being amongst the top five achievers over the last ten years, few of our games are on the television.

"That makes it difficult for players at this club who have international ambitions.

"At other clubs, if a player does well, the media get behind him and demand that he plays for his country. That has never happened at Forest.

"I really wanted to play a part in the 1996 European Championships and, with my chances of being picked by coach Terry Venables looking slim, I started to look at the alternatives.

"With the right kind of Welsh and Scottish background, I knew I had a chance of playing international football.

"Unfortunately, Frank Clark was not too keen on me declaring my allegiance to Wales or Scotland. As a foreigner, it would have caused problems with the UEFA Cup.

"Fortunately, the ruling was abolished half way into our cup run and I was free to make a choice. I decided to try Scotland.

"I sent off documents to the Scottish FA that proved my eligibility and was hoping to prove to Scotland coach, Craig Brown, that I was good enough for his Euro '96 plans.

"As the last English team in Europe that season, Forest began to enjoy a fair bit of publicity and I hoped that might help me clinch a spot in Craig Brown's plans.

"However, although he made encouraging noises in the beginning, I didn't get into his squad.

"Having spoken to my Forest team-mate and Scotland player, Scot Gemmill, it seems that Brown believed my England Under-21 caps precluded me from playing for any other country.

"All those caps, though, came in a friendly tournament in Toulon and, having personally checked with the English FA, I was free to play for other nations.

"I was desperate to join my understudy, Alan Fettis, on international duty. I was keeping him out of the Forest side, but he was an Northern Ireland international.

"I only wished I could find some Irish connection in my background!

"Of course, I still had a Welsh grandfather and decided to send certificates off to the Welsh FA to confirm my eligibility.

"Much to my relief, coach Bobby Gould decided to take a chance on me and I'm grateful for it.

"I knew it wouldn't be easy to force my way past Neville Southall to get the Number One shirt, but I was just happy to get the opportunity to link up with an international team.

"Having touted myself for other countries, I can understand why people might question whether I would give my all for Wales. They were wrong, though.

"Once I dedicate myself to a cause, that is it. I am now 100 per cent Welsh." ●

lucky!
1 2 3

JOACHIM

AFTER IMPRESSIVE spells in Norway with SK Brann Bergen and then Swedish cracks IFK Gothenburg, Joachim Bjorklund thought he'd really hit the big time when he moved to Serie A side Vicenza.

But, just a year after leaving Italy, Jocky now believes joining Rangers was the best move of his life — and he'd be happy to remain at Ibrox for the rest of his career!

The Swedish internationalist, a nephew of Sweden boss Tommy Svensson, reckons life with the perennial Scottish champs just gets better and better — but, when you've won the League for the past nine years, that's understandable.

However, it's not just the glory of lifting trophies and being involved in the European Champions League every year that has Jocky in dreamland. He also reckons Scotland is the nicest country he's lived in, too.

"I had heard so much about the cold weather here," admits the 26-year-old, "and people told me the food wasn't very good and that no Scottish club would ever be up there with the really top-class sides, like Juventus, Real Madrid, Barcelona, and Milan.

"But I have been stunned by the ambitions of Rangers, and I am surrounded by top-quality players. And, off the field, I just can't believe how passionate the supporters are.

"As for the food, I have found plenty of great Italian restaurants, who serve my favourite pasta dishes, so I'm certainly not going hungry!

"During my time with Vicenza, the stadium was half the size of Ibrox, and we struggled to fill it even against the top teams. The fans' passion was similar, but deep down we didn't realistically expect to win anything. UEFA Cup involvement would have been seen as a huge bonus — and a big surprise!

"Now I am having to adjust to the supporters EXPECTING us to win EVERYTHING — and just being in the Champions League each season isn't enough. They want us to WIN it.

"Eventually, I think we can, because there is unlimited money here and every close season more superstars are brought into the team.

"In fact, one big name was my countryman, Jonas Thern, who came from Roma, and he certainly added more quality to the side.

"Jonas is aggressive, can pass well, scores his fair share of goals, and most of all his name is respected — and feared — throughout the Continent. I admit I had a word with him to convince Jonas that Rangers would suit his style, but I know he had already decided to come here.

"Any player would want to play alongside men like Brian Laudrup and Paul Gascoigne and, with Jonas and others also joining up, the top clubs in Europe know we will soon be a handful for anyone."

Having tied up a ninth consecutive Premier Division Championship, and equalled the feat first attained by arch-rivals Celtic, Rangers gaffer Walter Smith was handed an incredible £40 million to spend in the summer.

But, though that kind of financial muscle looks sure to fire the Light Blues even further ahead of the men from Glasgow's East End, Jocky predicts that 1997-98 will be tougher than ever.

For, while new additions will continue to arrive to boost Rangers' squad, there have been departures, too — and Jocky has vowed to do everything in his power to fill the gap created when skipper Richard Gough left.

"Richard was a one-off, a man who lived for the club," admits the Swedish ace, "and he will be very hard to replace.

"He had great ability and read the game well, but he was also the fittest man at the club, and was totally professional. But we have players ready to fill that role, and we are all aware that a solid defence has always been a strong point for any Rangers team.

"It is true that Richard also scored a decent number of goals — particularly from set-pieces in vital matches, such as Europe.

"I rarely go up to the other end of the park, and I much prefer to be the man who stays back. Now, if I somehow found myself with a scoring chance, I'd probably not know what to do!

"Fortunately, though, Walter Smith is quite happy to let me hang back and, anyway, with Goughie gone it is even more important that I don't stray too far upfield.

"Also, we must never write off Celtic. They have really taken up the challenge in the past couple of seasons, and they, too, have brought some fine players to Scotland.

"Paolo di Canio, for example, is the kind of player every supporter must admire, and he is very tricky to play against. And I am sure Celtic will continue to spend big money to catch us.

"We experienced great pressure from them last season, because they were desperate to prevent us equalling nine-in-a-row. So you can imagine how hard they will try to stop us reaching ten and setting a new record! That makes for another very intriguing season."

One of Jocky's biggest matches of last season took place at Ibrox — but it wasn't for Rangers.

Bjorklund found himself in the odd position of playing for Sweden against Scotland at his club's home ground, one of the few times when he saw the VISITORS' dressing-room!

Scotland won 1-0 that day, but Jocky took revenge in the return in Gothenburg's Ullevi Stadium, when Sweden won convincingly — and he found himself up against Rangers team-mate Gordon Durie, who came on as a substitute.

But the Vaxjo-born defender laughs off the suggestion that it's very awkward to tackle hard against someone you have to work with every day.

"I admit I had slightly mixed feelings in those games — especially the one at Ibrox — because I would like to see BOTH countries reaching the 1998 World Cup Finals in France," Bjorklund explains.

"In Gothenburg, the patriotic home crowd helped me forget about my Scottish connection, and I played quite well. But you just have to be very professional, and forget your friendships, when you play against a club colleague.

"Gordon would feel the same way. You have to be single-minded about it, because, if you go into a tackle half-heartedly, you end up hurt. That's the type of attitude we must have about ten-in-a-row, and I'm sure we'll get it right." ●

> ## Just being in the Champions League isn't enough! They want us to WIN it!

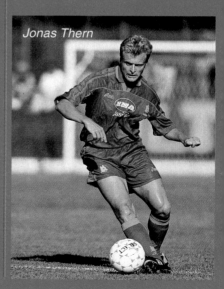

Jonas Thern

JOCKY!

BJORKLUND | likes the Rangers way of life!

ASTON VILLA **gareth** SOUTHGATE

it's a funny old game

Not many players are rushed to hospital after a clash with one of their team-mates but it happened to Jean-Luc Sassus of French club Lyons. He had an argument during a French League match with his goalkeeper Pascal Olmeta who promptly punched him. Sassus was stretchered off and taken to hospital with a suspected fractured jaw. On that same day earlier this year four other French players were sent off in League matches. It must have been one of those days . . .

Rod Stewart's son Liam is being raised as soccer daft as his dad. Not only did Rod have a full-size soccer pitch created in the grounds of his home in Essex but also gave Liam the second name of McAllister in honour of his pal Gary.

One of the biggest crowd attractions in Spain is a soccer team called Las Ibericas. They are a side composed entirely of Spanish actresses. They came together for a film in which they were a women's football team and enjoyed themselves so much they decided to keep it going for charity matches. Could catch on — watch out for Baywatch Rovers.

One of the first ever pitches used by Blackburn Rovers had a pond in the middle. Before each game the hole was covered with planks and soil was then scattered on top. Amazingly nobody ever went for an early bath although there must have been a few defeated teams who had that sinking feeling.

Forget the season of goodwill. There are just as many sendings-off and punch-ups around Christmas time as at any other time and often there are more. In 1990 there was even a sending-off world record established in Italy when Bologna's Giuseppe Lorenzo was dismissed after only ten seconds for dangerous play. He couldn't get an early bath, there hadn't even been time to put the plug in!

"I know our defence is leaking but this is rediculous!"

who's the BOSS?

That's a question often asked by Manchester City's

IAN BRIGHTWELL

CHARTING Ian Brightwell's career at Manchester City provides, perhaps, the best illustration of why the club has struggled so much in the last few years.

He signed his first professional contract at Maine Road for Billy McNeill in May 1986, but made his debut under Jimmy Frizzell's management a few months later.

He came to prominence, though, as Mel Machin's Second Division team achieved promotion back to the top division.

His most success-filled period followed under Machin's successor, Howard Kendall, as City looked to be establishing themselves as a force in the game. It was a similar story under player-boss Peter Reid.

Things took a turn for the worse, however, as Francis Lee's take-over as Chairman saw Ian's new 'gaffer', Brian Horton, struggle with a heavily reduced budget.

Next up was Alan Ball. After a horrendous start to his reign, City's relegation from the Premiership was inevitable — and so was Ball's sacking.

That was back in 1996 and what happened in the next few months was nothing short of amazing.

Caretaker-manager Asa Hartford was quickly replaced by Steve Coppell. 33 days later Coppell resigned.

Phil Neal was next to hold the fort, albeit on a temporary basis,

and, after just a few games in charge, he lost out to Frank Clark in the race to become the club's new permanent manager in December 1996.

That meant that Clark was Ian's 11th manager in ten-and-a-half years at Maine Road!

Considering such instability, it is amazing that one player should have remained in the Sky Blue colours for such a period of time.

For any player to exceed ten years at a single club is something. To do so at Manchester City is nothing short of a miracle.

Ian, though, has nothing but good memories of his time at the club.

"It is quite something to have served under so many managers," says the 29-year-old. "Perhaps I am a jinx on them!

"I served under four different ones last season alone. Even taking them out of the equation, though, I've still had my fair share of bosses.

"Managers need a few years to build a side. Unfortunately, not many recent City managers have had that opportunity.

"We needed stability and, in Frank Clark, that is what we got. His pedigree is good wherever he has been.

"I'm certainly hopeful that we are on our way back to enjoying some good times at the club. It

> There was talk a few years ago of Leeds and Arsenal being interested in signing me but then I got injured and was out for a year. Perhaps it was fated that I stay at Maine Road.

find a manager, just a few weeks later, there was even greater unrest. Unbelievable!

"Some people have said that I should have left but I've never seen the need. I've never been asked to go and that is fine by me.

"A lot of players I grew up with at City left for pastures new. David White left to go to Leeds but moved on, Steve Redmond went to Oldham, and Andy Hinchcliffe had a lot of problems before his move to Everton became a success.

"So, all in all, I don't think my career has suffered by remaining at City.

"There was talk a few years ago of Leeds and Arsenal being interested in signing me but then I was injured and was out for a year. Perhaps it was fated that I stay at Maine Road.

"I'm 29 now and want to be here when the club starts to win things. With Frank Clark in charge, I'm confident that will be soon.

"We had good spells under Howard Kendall and Peter Reid a few years back and looked like we could challenge for things. They were good times and we have the potential to get back to that level." ●

may surprise people, but I have had a few at City.

"I've seen the good and not so good times. I would never say bad times because I've never not wanted to come in to train or play.

"I've had ups and downs like most players. The only difference is that you seem to get more of them at Manchester City.

"It may sound strange but it has been a pleasure to have been here. The way I look at it is that I would not have had so many experiences anywhere else.

"Some of things that have gone on have been really funny. I look back now and think, 'That could only happen at Manchester City.'

"For example, it was really sad when Steve Coppell left after such a short period of time through ill health.

"After all that time searching to

83

MANCHESTER CITY fan Philip Noble is not your ordinary football fan.

Over the years, he has collected prized cup final programmes, autographs and pictures.

Just don't ask him, though, to name his favourite possession — he has literally thousands to choose from!

His bedroom is a testament to over a decade of attending collectors' fairs, browsing through catalogues and answering advertisements. Every inch of wall and ceiling has Manchester City memorabilia hanging from it.

There are countless shelves full of programmes carefully preserved in specially made folders. There are old season ticket books, flags, shirts, letters and City handkerchiefs. He even has an old bench from City's Platt Lane stand!

With everything carefully indexed and respectfully looked after, a visit to Philip's room is just like taking in a trip to a museum. And with his comprehensive knowledge of City's history, he makes an excellent curator.

Why Manchester City fan PHILIP NOBLE needs to build an extension!

Says Philip, "I decided half-way through the 1985/86 season to keep the programmes from the games I was attending and it snowballed from there.

"City used to sell the away programmes in their souvenir shop and once I started buying them, I was hooked.

"I now have every City home programme from the 1946/47 season onwards and I'm missing less than ten away programmes from the same period. I'm now working backwards from the Second World War.

"I have all the programmes from City's cup final appearances and, in some cases, I have the match ticket, train ticket and after-match banquet menu as well!

"The memorabilia side started about five years ago and that is something I'm beginning to develop more and more.

"My oldest pieces are a fixture list from the 1899-1900 season and a club crest badge which dates from the early 1890s.

"The more unusual ones include a passport of Billy Dale, who was an old City player, and the bench.

"The club doesn't have any collection of its own and they've been really helpful to me. Every time someone writes to the club offering things, they forward it to me.

"As my collection has grown, it has become more and more difficult to get the programmes I'm missing and I'm having to search further and harder than ever. Just recently I received some things from a lady 12,000 miles away in Australia!

"The one big problem I have is that my room just isn't big enough to show everything. I've drawers full of things that should be shown.

"Perhaps if City read this, they will make room for a museum and I'll run it for them. That would be my dream job!" ●

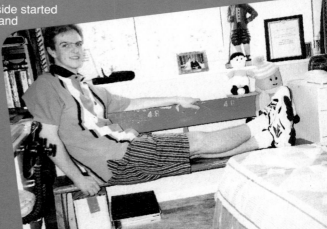

dean
SAUNDERS

It's a **soccer** feast at football foo

● Collector and historian Bryan Horsnell invited the Topical Times on a whistle-stop tour of FOOTBALL FOOTBALL, the theme restaurant and museum in central London.

● Have a snack or a meal and watch live football from any one of dozens of TV screens . . . then buy a souvenir from the restaurant's well-stocked shop.

● Geoff Hurst's 1966 World Cup Final shirt.

BROWNS CLUB LONDON

● Many players have donated international and club jerseys to the display. Here's Bryan with shirts from Jurgen Klinsmann and Maradona — and there are lots, lots more.

tball

● George Best and Geoff Hurst have donated several items to the museum. Trophies, caps, boots . . . even their footprints!

● Geoff's cap and Man-of-the-Match trophy from the 1966 World Cup Final.

● The George Best case, containing the Football Writers' Footballer of the Year award, European Footballer of the Year trophy, Northern Ireland cap, Manchester United Silver Jubilee shirt . . . and his first-ever football boots!

● The museum also boasts pennants, badges, medals, caps, trophies and other memorabilia which make it a treasure trove of football history for football fans young and old.

● FOOTBALL FOOTBALL is in London's Haymarket and is a must for any football fan passing through the capital. You could spend hours wandering through the displays. We certainly did!

local he

There's no place like home for Sheffield
JON NEWSOME

I T took five years for Jon Newsome's career to turn full circle when he returned to his hometown club, Sheffield Wednesday, in March, 1995.

Unfortunately for the defender, it took almost a year to settle into the side which he supported as a youngster.

Following his £1.5 million move from Norwich City, the former Leeds United man was plunged straight into a relegation battle and helped his new club retain their Premiership status.

However, just as he was preparing for a new campaign and a chance to establish himself at Hillsborough, injury struck. A damaged tendon, which finally required surgery, meant he took almost a year to reach double

figures in terms of first-team appearances.

No sooner had he done so than he dislocated an ankle and had to sit out the remainder of the season.

Throughout the frustration of his on-

off injury, however, Newsome was always grateful that he had come back to a club where the emphasis was on football rather than behind-the-scenes politics, the situation which marred his two years at Carrow Road.

Jon explains, "When I went to Norwich from Leeds, I thought it was a good move. I thought they were similar to Sheffield Wednesday a few years ago in that they probably wouldn't win the League, but were good enough to hold on in the Premiership.

"But after a few months, the circumstances changed. There was a lot of to-ing and fro-ing involving the Board and the managers. In less than two years with the club, I played under four different managers. One of those, Gary Megson, actually had two spells in charge.

"At the end of that first season, we were relegated and, considering the amount of chopping and changing which was taking place, it was not surprising that the team suffered.

"It was a shame, because I liked the club and the area. But there was a lot of speculation at that time about my future with the club.

"I kept reading stories in the newspapers that it was only a matter of time before I would be leaving.

"Although I never allowed that to unsettle me on the field, it was unsettling for my family. We lived in rented accommodation for the first year, and never quite knew whether we should take the plunge and buy a house.

"At the end of that season, however, I was called in to see the Chairman, Robert Chase. He told me that the club had received offers for me, but he had categorically turned them down, telling the prospective buyers that I would not be allowed to leave Carrow Road.

"That suited me. I'd had no intention of seeking a transfer. I felt that, as I had been a member of the team which had taken the club down into the First Division, it would be a very poor show if I said that I wanted to leave.

"That discussion with the Chairman also gave me the confidence to buy a house and try to become more settled in the area."

Nine months later, however, the Newsomes were on the move as the Norwich supremo did an about-turn.

"I was called in to see Mr Chase again," Jon recalls. "This time, he told me that Sheffield Wednesday had made an offer and he had accepted it.

"By then, I was more ready to leave as Norwich was no longer such a pleasant place to play football.

"This was mainly because the fans had become very disgruntled with the way the Chairman was running things and most of the focus was on things happening off the pitch.

"To their credit, the fans never turned their frustrations on the players. Their loyalty, along with the feeling that I had been part of a family club and that it was a lovely part of the country to live in, made me sad to leave.

"But I was delighted to return to Hillsborough, where I served my apprenticeship and made my League debut.

"It has been good to once again be part of a club where the most important thing is what happens on a Saturday. Everything revolves around whether the team ends up with a win, a draw or a defeat and all the talk is about whether we can build on a run of victories or recover from a bad spell.

"At Norwich, all the conversation seemed to concentrate on what the Chairman was saying one day and whether he would be saying the same thing tomorrow.

"As a local lad who had a season ticket at Hillsborough before becoming a professional, I feel as though I have come home, even though it is much earlier than I expected.

"Although I began my career here, I always had the idea that I would probably move around a lot before returning to Sheffield. As this is such a short career, I knew that, if I had to move to the other end of the country in order to improve myself, then I would.

"Wherever I ended up, I am certain I would have returned to Sheffield eventually. I am delighted to have done so earlier than I expected, because I now have a chance to win something with my own club.

"When I was a member of Leeds United's Championship-winning side in 1991, it was a superb experience. But, at 19, I was probably too young to appreciate how big an achievement that was.

"My team-mate, Steve Hodge, was near to the end of his playing career and told me, 'Take everything in and savour all you can. You don't know how long you will have to wait before this comes round again.'

"I tried to heed his words, but did not appreciate at the time exactly how right he was. I only played in the last quarter of that season, and my impression was the wrong one.

"At the age of 19 and having only just broken into the team, I found myself playing in a side that was winning every week. I thought this was the norm.

"The following season, when we did not do so well, it was like a poke in the eye.

"If I am ever in that trophy-winning situation again, I will certainly make the most of it. I'd like to think that might be with Sheffield Wednesday." ●

> **I was more ready to leave as Norwich was no longer such a pleasant place to play football.**

Newsome with Leeds ... and Norwich

BELL'S PREMIER DIVISION WINNERS SEASON 96/97

getting
even!

Where it all began. Rangers' Championship - winning side in 1989

WEDNESDAY MAY 7th, 1997. That's a date I, and everyone else connected with Rangers, will never forget.

On that day, by beating Dundee United 1-0 at Tannadice, we finally clinched our ninth successive Championship, equalling Celtic's long-held record.

Every single person connected with the club was overjoyed but for me, in particular, it was a very emotional occasion.

That's because I was convinced I'd BLOWN my chance to take part in the historic nine-in-a-row-clinching campaign!

During the previous season, I'd decided that the time was right for me to move on from Ibrox, and I joined up with my old team-mate Ray Wilkins at QPR.

I'd been going through a period where I was constantly struggling with injuries and just couldn't seem to find my best form.

I was feeling really down and felt I had to get away even though, in hindsight, I realise I should never have left Ibrox.

But when things are going badly for you, you sometimes make rash decisions and that's exactly what I did.

So I had to suffer a NIGHTMARE spell at Loftus Road.

Because of the situation the club was in at the time, with a real lack of strikers, I was playing from the start even though I was a long way short of match fitness.

That meant my performances weren't up to my usual standard, and because of that the fans were getting on my back.

So to try and regain my form and fitness, Ray agreed to let me go on loan to Leeds at the start of the 1996/97 season.

But, at Elland Road, the team were struggling, and Ian Rush and I just couldn't seem to strike up a

90

scoring partnership.

So I ended up back at QPR.

To make matters worse, I was constantly scanning all the English papers to find out how Rangers were getting on in their quest to clinch that vital ninth title!

And, of course, Ally McCoist was on the phone regularly talking about how well things were going — for him, that is!

Little did I know, then, that I would be back at my beloved Ibrox, playing my OWN part in a history-making season, and having to put up with Ally again, within a few weeks!

But, as soon as I heard that Walter Smith wanted to bring me back, I didn't exactly have to think it over.

In fact, I was in my Ferrari and back up the M1 before I'd even had time to pack!

And the main reason for that was my desperation to be part of the nine-in-a-row celebrations.

Ever since I arrived at the club back in the summer of 1990, there was a real belief that we could match the achievement of Jock Stein's great Celtic side of the '60s and '70s.

It was something that guys like Richard Gough, Ian Ferguson and Ian Durrant, Rangers men to the core, were completely focused on.

Ever since 1990, there was a real belief that we could match the achievement of Jock Stein's great Celtic side of the '60s and '70s.

They made sure that new arrivals like myself, from England, knew EXACTLY what it meant to reach that target.

So I knew full well the importance of helping us get a result in my first game back in the Light Blue, last March.

This just happened to be a friendly little Old Firm clash in front of 50,000 fanatical fans at Parkhead in what was billed as the 'title decider'!

Celtic had just beaten us in the Cup and were determined to stop us equalling their cherished record.

It was undoubtedly one of the biggest games of my career.

And it was CERTAINLY one of the most eventful!

I managed to get the flick-on that set up Brian Laudrup for what proved to be the winner.

But my day took a turn for the worse when I was sent off for a 'nothing' incident involving Celtic 'keeper Stewart Kerr.

It was handbags-at-ten-paces stuff, but for some reason the referee decided I had to go.

I spent the rest of the game biting my nails on the bench but fortunately the lads dug in tremendously, despite my dismissal and Richard Gough's injury, to earn a hard-fought win.

Those three points virtually ensured we'd clinch nine-in-a-row, but it wasn't until that Wednesday in May against Dundee United that we could REALLY start celebrating!

Now, having achieved nine-in-a-row and currently bidding to make it ten, I know comparisons will be made between us and the Celtic side that dominated Scottish football under Jock Stein.

What I would say is that it certainly isn't any easier to win Championships these days.

I've won seven of them here and each one has been hard-earned.

Celtic fans will no doubt claim that the standard of Scottish football generally was higher during 1965-74.

I disagree.

The advent of the Premier League has meant that there are NO easy games any more.

With only nine other sides in the Division, there are no easy touches.

Every team has something to play for, whether it's a European place, going for the title or trying to avoid relegation.

That means every game is fiercely contested and every victory hard-earned.

Was that really the case for Celtic in the old 18-team First Division?

And, while Celtic achieved the ultimate prize of winning the European Cup, we, too, have had our moments in Europe.

During the 1992-93 Champions League campaign, we came within a whisker of reaching the Final ourselves, only to be pipped at the post by eventual winners Marseille.

That was despite the punishing domestic campaign that season, in which we played a lot more games than teams from the sixties and seventies had to.

People will argue forever about which nine-in-a-row side was better but, at the end of the day, we'll never really know.

What IS certain, however, is that winning nine titles in a row, in ANY era, is an astonishing achievement.

■ *Unfortunately Mark's return to Ibrox was brief. He was released by Rangers in the close season.*

■ *And where it ended. Brian Laudrup's goal against Dundee United which sealed the nine-in-a-row.*

past masters!

TOMMY GEMMELL!

RANGERS did incredibly well to equal our famous nine-in-a-row record last season and I was the first to congratulate them.

But they cannot be compared to the Celtic side that first reached that landmark UNTIL they emulate us and win the ultimate prize — the European Cup.

That's the real benchmark of a great side and, until the 'Gers achieve that, they'll always be second best, no matter how many League titles they win.

But before I'm accused of sour grapes, let me first pay tribute to Walter Smith's side.

To maintain that level of consistency is astonishing and, given the number of changes there have been in the side, it's an even more remarkable achievement.

With the exception of guys like Richard Gough and Ally McCoist, who seem to have been around forever, the team that clinched the nine-in-a-row is virtually

unrecognisable from that which won the first title.

Walter Smith, and Graeme Souness before him, constantly rung the changes and that helped keep the team fresh.

By bringing in new players who were hungry for success, they ensured that the appetite for honours among the players remained constant.

That was the same trick that big Jock Stein used when we were enjoying our record run.

Since imitation is the sincerest form of flattery, I suppose it's a great compliment to our Celtic side!

But, seriously, Rangers have completely dominated the domestic scene for the best part of a decade and deserve full credit for it.

However, having had a relatively easy ride in the Premier Division, there is no excuse for their abject failure in Europe.

When we were winning our League Championships between 1965 and 1974, we were invariably pushed right to the last game or two by Rangers or Aberdeen.

In 1967, the year we won the European Cup in Lisbon, we had to get a result against Rangers at Ibrox or else they could have taken the title.

We drew 2-2 and won the point we needed to secure the title, with Jimmy Johnstone popping up with a double, including an unstoppable 25-yarder with his left foot.

That was an example of how hard we had to battle for our success.

By contrast, with the exception of Aberdeen one season, and Celtic in the last couple of campaigns, Rangers have ROMPED to the title virtually unchallenged.

Which makes their European failure all the more puzzling.

The Celtic sides which I was fortunate enough to play in were constantly reaching the latter stages of the European Cup.

After from winning the trophy itself on that glorious Lisbon evening in '67, we reached the Final again in '70.

In '72, we went out on penalties in the semi-final and we reached the last four again in 1974, by which time I'd left for Dundee.

When you add in our two quarter-final appearances as well, you can see that we were always there or thereabouts when it came to the European Cup.

But it wasn't just Celtic who were causing the Continentals a problem or two in these days.

Rangers were also a force to be reckoned with in Europe.

They, like us, reached two major European finals, in the Cup-Winners' Cup competition.

In fact, just a week after big Billy McNeill lifted the European Cup in Lisbon, Rangers narrowly went down 1-0 to Bayern Munich in Germany in the Cup-Winners' Cup.

Both halves of the Old Firm featured in European finals within a week of each other!

Nowadays, we'd be celebrating if both of them managed to win a GAME in Europe.

That's proof of the poorer standard of the game in Scotland.

With the exception of 1992-93, when they produced some terrific performances against the likes of Leeds and Marseille, the Gers seem to have gone backwards in terms of European competition.

Embarrassing exits at the hands of AEK Athens and Levski Sofia, combined with humiliating hammerings from quality outfits like Juventus and Ajax, show just how far we lag behind the Continentals.

That's not just a criticism of Rangers' displays because Celtic have suffered just as badly, if not worse.

But it does show that the overall standard of the Scottish game is far lower than it was when we racked up title after title.

Some pundits claim that the problem stems from our players having too many games to play and that the standard inevitably suffers because of that.

The season that ended with us lifting the European Cup saw us win every competition we entered.

That campaign we played 65 games.

And, when you consider that the majority of us were also featuring regularly for our international side, most players could play up to 70 matches!

That's two games a week, every week of the season!

We didn't complain. In fact we preferred it!

Playing matches was, and is, preferable to the hard slog of training.

So there's no reason why the modern professional should be complaining about the number of games he has to play.

Rangers have relied heavily on non-Scots throughout their nine-in-a-row, whereas Celtic's squad was firmly home-based.

Terry Butcher and Chris Woods were two of Graeme Souness's first, and best, signings.

While Walter Smith has come to rely heavily on the talents of Rangers' Great Dane Brian Laudrup and the brilliant, if erratic, Paul Gascoigne.

In Jock Stein's Celtic side, we all thought Bobby Lennox was a bit exotic because he came from Saltcoats — 30 miles from Glasgow!

Rangers nine-in-a-row has also been made possible thanks to the financial muscle of Chairman David Murray.

For the first six years of Rangers' record run, the Murray millions put the 'Gers in a different financial League to the rest of Scottish football.

> **They'll always be second best, no matter how many League titles they win.**

■ *Billy McNeil and Bobby Lennox took part in all of Celtic's nine-in-a-row Championships.*

The arrival of Fergus McCann, Celtic's Scots-Canadian Chairman, has seen the gap narrow greatly, with Celtic now competing in the same multi-million pound marketplace as their great rivals.

Some things never change.

When I was playing for Celtic, Rangers were the megabucks club even then.

But thanks to the genius of Jock Stein, and the talent of the players he nurtured, we achieved our nine-in-a-row despite that hurdle.

I suppose that the best way to settle the issue of which nine-in-a-row team was best would be to have them play each other.

I think it would be an extremely close game, almost impossible to predict.

But, bear in mind, all of our Celtic side are over 50 now!

Seriously, though, both sides would undeniably be top-class in any era.

But, man-for-man, I think our side had the greater individual talent and an astonishing team-spirit — and we have the European Cup medals to prove it! ●

■ *Jock Stein.*

BLACKBURN ROVERS kevin GALLACHER

NEWCASTLE UNITED alan SHEARER

making his mark!

Most defences know they've been in a game if they've faced Chelsea's ace striker Mark Hughes!

crossword

across

6. Matt Le ———- (7)
7. Barry, a Souness player in Turkey and at Southampton (7)
9. Millwall's ground (3)
10. Swindon player boss Steve (7)
11. Part of leg protected by pads (4)
12. Midfielder Mr Curcic (4)
15. Everton's young striking star Michael (6)
17. Torments a defender or cooks in the oven! (6)
18. Stadium, sporting venue (5)
20. Coventry's defender Daish (4)
23. Team beaten by Middlesbrough in the 1997 Coca-Cola semis (9, 6)
25. Boss Bassett (4)
26. Team from Stark's Park (5)
28. Dmitri Kharine's country (6)
30. Spurs ace Anderton (6)
31. The Wembley turf is said to do this to a player's strength (4)
33. An outfield player cannot use these to control the ball (4)
35. Long-serving Man Utd utility player Brian (7)
36. England keeper Flowers (3)
38. Kinkladze's country (7)
39. Tottenham veteran defender Gary (7)

24. Found on the underside of boots (5)
27. Alex Ferguson and Roy Aitken have managed this team (8)
29. City team from Glebe Park (7)

32. Southampton's nickname (6)
34. Italian city that Paul Ince moved to (5)
37. Boss Barry of Barnet, Birmingham and Peterborough (3)

down

1. Nickname for Hull (6)
2. Swansea's Field (5)
3. Come back off the bar or post (7)
4. Playing gear (3)
5. Everton's Park (8)
8. Italian striker who cost Middlesbrough £7 million (8, 9)
11. Item of kit that 8 down covers his face with after scoring (5)
13. Call off a match already started (7)
14. The opposite of defends (7)
16. Sell a player to another club (8)
19. Sky TV expert and former Scottish international striker (4, 4)
21. Red and white are Man Utd's (7)
22. Celebration party, especially in London's East End (5, 2)

it's a funny old game

John Hartson, ex-Arsenal, now West Ham, makes good use of the corner flag after taking exception to a Ravanelli tackle!

EYES... ...RIGHT!

No! It's still there, Ian. Razor Ruddock hasn't shaved it off.

I know you said to come early for a decent seat, but two months is a bit too much!

Now, Glenn Hoddle just played Mr Bun the Baker. If I play . . .

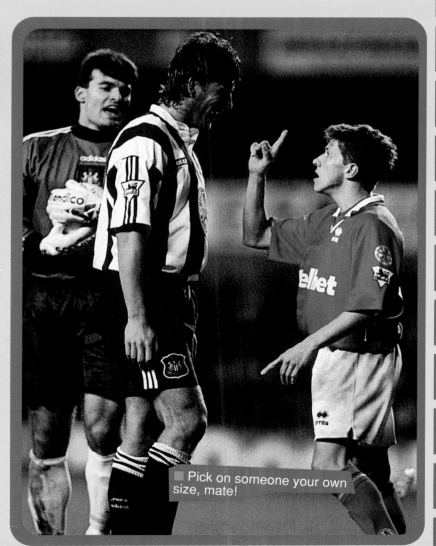

Pick on someone your own size, mate!

thankd

EAN STURRIDGE OWES A DEBT TO TORQUAY!

MOST footballers will tell you that the Premiership is the only place to play. It has everything going for it — the money, the glamour clubs, the best grounds, biggest crowds and massive media coverage.

Dean Sturridge has lapped it all up since Derby County gained promotion to the elite two seasons ago. Like most schoolboys, he dreamed of performing at Old Trafford, Anfield and Highbury.

Yet he would be the first to tell you that the Premiership is not the be-all and end-all. He knows from experience that the 72 Nationwide League clubs fulfil an equally important role.

Just two years ago, Sturridge's Derby career looked to be heading nowhere.

Having joined the club as an apprentice, he had made just 11 appearances by the age of 21 and had yet to notch a goal. In the queue of big-name, expensive forwards searching for a striking role at the club, he was easily jostled to the back.

Enter Third Division Torquay United.

Five goals in ten loan appearances later, and Dean found himself a wanted man by Derby's new manager, Jim Smith.

The rest, as they say, is history.

Says the 24-year-old, "I wouldn't be where I am now if it wasn't for Torquay United. If I'd turned that loan move down, I could well have still been stuck in the reserves at Derby.

"To be honest, though, I had no choice but to try and prove myself in the Third Division. I wasn't exactly a young first-year professional. It was a case of now or never for me.

"I had to face facts. I was 21, the fifth choice striker, and Derby were happy to see me go on loan to Torquay. The future did not look bright.

"Everything changed when I temporarily moved to the South coast. I was a regular first teamer and was scoring goals. It was a real education.

"At Derby, I was in awe of the likes of Paul Simpson, Marco Gabbiadini and Tommy Johnson. They, in my eyes, were big stars.

"That meant that if I got a game, I was just delighted if I came off the pitch having not made a mistake. I just didn't want to let anyone down.

"It was only when I went to Torquay that I realised my job was to score goals. I wasn't there to link up play and look pretty — I was in the team to hit the back of the net.

"It was the first time that I really got a buzz from seeing the ball fly past the goalkeeper. It was fantastic.

"I'd never lost faith in my ability but that spell hardened my attitude to the game. I became much more focused and thrived on goals.

"When I returned to Derby at the end of the loan, there was still a lot of work to do. I still wasn't certain of a first team place.

"That was made quite clear from the early match programmes of Derby's promotion year. Between August and September, my face wasn't even on the page which listed the players' kit sponsors!

"Fortunately, Jim Smith replaced Roy McFarland as manager and he wiped the slate clean for me. He told me me to prove my worth to him and Derby.

"For the first time, I got a run in the side, scored a few goals and even managed to get my mug-shot in the programme. I was still the only one without a sponsor, though!

"But as I continued to score goals, that soon changed and my profile went up. I put that down almost solely to playing in the Third Division with Torquay.

"Jim Smith summed up the change that period brought about in me when he started to have a go at me for having a scowl on my face because I hadn't scored for a couple of games.

"Before I tasted life at Torquay, I would have thought nothing of going six games without hitting the target."

Last season saw Dean make a real impact on the game. He was one of the success stories of the campaign as his goals helped Derby, whom many had tipped for relegation, more than cope with the added demands of top flight football.

The now super-focused goal-getter, though, believes he was a bit of a let-down.

He knows he has a long, long way to go before he can consider himself worthy of mention alongside his idol, Ian Wright.

He goes on, "I didn't score as many as I should have done. That was disappointing.

"People said that I was being hard on myself considering it was my first year at that level but I didn't see it that way. I should have done better.

"My aim was to make an impression so that people sat up and took notice of me. I went some way towards that, but not as far as I'd hoped.

"That was best illustrated after the final whistle of the game at Arsenal.

"My idol is Ian Wright. I love his attitude and often spend time watching videos of his games. I know there is a lot I can learn from him.

"I desperately wanted to swop shirts with him. It would have been the ultimate souvenir.

"Unfortunately, he didn't play ball. He told me that Arsenal's kit manager was quite strict about getting the shirts back after the game and he couldn't risk giving it to me.

"I don't know for sure, but I reckon he was giving me the brush-off.

"Would Ian Wright really have wanted a Dean Sturridge shirt? Next to all the shirts and souvenirs he must have collected, my Derby shirt wouldn't have been too impressive.

"It just goes to show how far I've got to go before I can say "I've made it." There are plenty of improvements to make.

"That process started as soon as I got into the Premiership. My all-round game has come on in leaps and bounds.

"In the First Division, I just used to get the ball, turn, and run at defenders. I quickly learned that I couldn't do that all the time in the Premiership. I've had to time when to release the ball and when to run with it.

"The biggest thing I need now, though, is experience. I'm still a youngster in terms of top level football and my best years are ahead of me.

"Whatever happens, though, I will still look back to the time spent at Torquay as the most crucial of my career." ●

"Okay, Dean. You CAN have my shirt..."

"... and you might as well have my boots as well!"

evon!

LIVERPOOL robbie FOWLER

Good times? Bad times? ask CRAIG HIGNETT what they're like!

CRAIG HIGNETT knows all about the ups-and-downs of a professional footballer. The Middlesbrough man seems to experience them every season!

The 27-year-old has seen it all with 'Boro. Relegation, promotion, Ayresome Park and the Riverside Stadium, multi-million pound signings and Wembley cup finals.

However, the man who arrived from Crewe for £500,000 in 1992 has been on the verge of leaving Middlesbrough more often than the team bus! It has virtually become a summer ritual for Hignett to worry about his future.

Despite being at the club for over five years, the Liverpudlian midfielder has rarely felt like an established first-team regular. But he has still managed to outstay some of the bigger names who have been at the club.

He admits, however, that there were times when he felt as though he was fighting a losing battle.

Says Craig, "I have always survived at Middlesbrough when it seemed that I would be on my way. There have been numerous occasions when it appeared that I would leaving.

"The first time was back in the days of former manager Lennie Lawrence. Lennie brought me to the club, but I hardly played in the role that he bought me to play—behind the front two, and eventually he put me up for transfer.

"He tried to sell me to Bradford City, who were in the Second Division, but I didn't want to go. I stuck to my guns and stayed at 'Boro and at the end of that season Lennie was sacked. Ironically, he took over at Bradford!

"When Bryan Robson succeeded Lennie, it seemed as though I would be on my way again. Bryan put me on the transfer list in his first season at the club, but there were no takers and I ended up staying.

"I was out of contract, but the club had just been promoted to the Premiership and were about to move into the Riverside Stadium. I didn't want to pass up the chance of playing in the Premiership, so I took a pay cut to stay at the club.

"When I did that, it was always with the intention of doing enough to earn myself a new deal. The club had just signed Nick Barmby from Spurs and the manager paired us together in midfield.

"We hit it off straightaway and put in some great performances. Everybody was happy and after three months, the club offered me a new contract and I signed.

"That was the last good thing that happened to me that season. As soon as I signed the contract, I picked up a hernia injury and that cost me my place. If that wasn't bad enough, the club bought Juninho while I was out, so my chances of getting back into the side took a knock.

"I didn't get my place back that season. After starting so well, I ended up being out of the team because I couldn't shift either Nick or Juninho. At the end of that campaign I thought about my future and asked for a transfer.

"I wasn't playing regularly and was nearly 27. I believed that I had to start thinking about what lay ahead and felt that it would be best to go somewhere else.

"If it wasn't for a few disagreements, I would probably have signed for Wolves. I was all set to go to Molineux, but things fell down at the last minute and I ended up staying at 'Boro. I'm glad I did.

"Apart from Wolves, nobody else really showed any interest. I could have gone to French club Strasbourg on loan, but Bryan Robson wouldn't let me go and that was that. I'm grateful to him for keeping me here because he sold Nick Barmby to Everton shortly

oaster ride!

afterwards and I was put back in the team.

"From the moment I played against Derby at the beginning of November, I gradually won my place back in the team. I ended up keeping my place and played in two cup finals, so it turned out to be a great year for me.

"I sometimes think that I still have to prove myself to the gaffer and win him over properly. When I'm left out, I wonder if he appreciates what I do. He knows what he wants, though, and when he has made mistakes in the past he has been fair enough to admit it."

Hignett admits that times were hard when he was forced to watch from the sidelines, unable to shift the likes of Barmby, Juninho and Emerson from the first-team.

He credits his former manager at Crewe, Dario Gradi, for keeping his spirits up and making sure he remained at the forefront of everybody's mind within the game.

Craig adds, "It wasn't easy when I was left out of the side because I would look at the lads in my place and wonder how I was going to force my way back in. There were times when I didn't want to come in in the mornings and just stay at home. I was fed up.

"Fortunately, I love football and when I have the ball at my feet in training, everything is forgotten. I used to get my frustrations out of my system just by kicking a ball in training. Looking back, that was the best thing to do.

"I also spoke to Dario Gradi quite a lot and he was very helpful. He reminded me that I had what it takes, but he would also send people up to watch me play in reserve games.

"Thanks to Dario, people within the game knew my situation and I was always being watched by somebody. It's always good to know that somebody out there is keeping an eye on you.

"David Platt, John Pemberton, Rob Jones and Geoff Thomas are all the same as me in that they keep in touch with Dario. Having all played for him at Crewe, we all know how much he did for us.

"It's nice that I'm now bracketed with the likes of Platty, Rob and Geoff when people talk about Crewe. It marks the progress I have made, but to stay in that bracket permanently I have to make sure I continue to do well."

> **There were times when I didn't want to come in in the mornings and just stay at home.**

getting to grips!

Nottingham Forest's Des Lyttle battles it out with Clive Wilson, Spurs

JAMIE POLLOCK played a key role in helping Bolton Wanderers make a swift return to the Premiership last season, but the former Middlesbrough midfielder could very nearly have spent the whole of the campaign in Spain!

At the end of the 1995-96 season, Pollock felt that he had to leave Middlesbrough, his home-town club and the team he supported as a boy, for the sake of his career.

Despite being a mere 22 years old, Pollock had seen six seasons of first-team action with the Teesside club. Even the high-profile arrivals of foreign stars like Fabrizio Ravanelli and Emerson could not convince him to stay at the club.

Once he became available, it seemed the former England Under-21 man would have no problems finding a new club. Several Premiership clubs were linked with Pollock, but when nothing came of their interest, he decided to try his luck abroad.

Along with Rob Ullathorne, now at Leicester City, Pollock signed for Spanish Second Division club Osasuna — but he was back in England before he had chance to get a suntan!

Jamie recalls, "I was in my seventh year at Middlesbrough and had never known anything different. I needed a new challenge and I am very grateful to everybody at Middlesbrough for letting me go.

"Sometimes you think you are settled for life at one place and that applied to me at Boro. When I realised I needed to leave it was a difficult decision, but I had to do what was best for my career.

"Middlesbrough were booming at the time, signing world stars like Ravanelli and Juninho, but I still felt I had to move on. Manager Bryan Robson was fantastic with me and totally understood my feelings.

"I wanted to stay in England and it seemed I would because there were links with Arsenal and Aston Villa. Nothing materialised, but my confidence wasn't affected because I knew that clubs wanted me. The deals just didn't seem to come off.

"When Osasuna came in, I jumped at the move because it was an attractive offer and I felt that a spell in Spain would be good for my career. Bryan Robson told me that it was a good club who had bought English players in the past, so I happily signed for them.

"It didn't work out, though. I was only there for two months during which time I made only one appearance as a substitute. If Bolton hadn't come in for me, however, I would have stuck it out in Spain.

"I was out there with my fiancee and we were trying hard to make a go of the move. However, while my time was taken up with the football, Lindsey was stuck in a hotel with nothing to do all day and it was difficult for her.

"When I decided to go to Spain, I knew it was only for one year. I believed it would be an invaluable experience, but I soon realised that the Spanish Second Division wasn't going to improve my game that much.

"I did learn a lot about fitness and enjoyed the different culture and lifestyle, but I missed English football. I would watch Premiership matches on TV and wish I was playing.

"Although I was willing to stay in Spain, I still had ambitions to come home, but only to the right club. When Bolton came in for me, I was happy to sign for them because I knew they were a club with a bright future.

"Osasuna were good with the transfer. I think they realised, like I did, that I wasn't a continental-type player. They let me go, but I had to sign for Middlesbrough again before I joined Bolton!

"One of the complications of the Bosman ruling meant I had to re-sign for Boro, who would then sell me to Bolton. Because I left Boro on good terms, there were no problems.

"I have no regrets about my time in Spain. The two months I had out there taught me a lot." ●

home wins!

There was no gain in Spain for Bolton's JAMIE POLLOCK!

> I was only there for two months during which time I made only one appearance as a substitute.

the wonder of W

For most players, playing at Wembley is the pinnacle of their careers. To walk out on to the hallowed turf is the stuff dreams are made of. But Wembley — the scene of some of football's greatest moments — is due for a major facelift. We thought we'd take the chance to reflect on some of the memories that have helped make Wembley the most famous football ground in the world.

We're sure every football fan has his or her own memory of Wembley. We're just sorry we can't print them all!

1 The first-ever FA Cup Final at Wembley, 1923 — the famous White Horse Final. A reported crowd of 200,000 forced their way in. When the crowd spilled on to the pitch, mounted police patiently eased them back, most notably PC George Scorey on his white horse, Billy. Incidentally, the final score was Bolton 2 — West Ham 0.

2 Wembley has hosted many England v Scotland fixtures, probably the oldest and most famous international match in the world. Although England hold the upper hand in recent encounters, Scotland more than held their own in the early years. This is the 1928 fixture where Scotland's Wembley Wizards won 5-1.

3 1963, the first of five Wembley European Cup Finals. Benfica's Eusebio comes close, but his team eventually lost out to AC Milan, 2-1.

4 Probably the most famous Wembley event ever. England's Bobby Moore with the 1966 World Cup.

5 Cup Final magic has always had its place in Wembley folklore. Five 'Doubles' have been won there — by Spurs, Arsenal, Liverpool and two by Manchester United. This is Charlie George's winner for Arsenal in 1971.

6 Coventry 3 — Spurs 2. Keith Houchen notches City's second goal with a glorious diving header.

7 History was made in 1988 when Wimbledon's Dave Beasant became the first keeper to save an FA Cup Final penalty. Beasant also captained the Dons to a 1-0 win over much-fancied Liverpool.

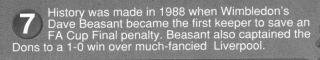

Turn over the page to see the new-look Wembley.

euro 96 England   euro 96 England   euro 96 England

the new look

The old stadium will be demolished, with only the famous twin towers remaining. In its place will rise a £180 million stadium, seating 80,000. Work is due to be completed by the year 2000.

● Artists' impressions

it's a funny old game

When the USA were playing in the first World Cup Finals in 1930 their trainer had to be carried off on a stretcher! He had rushed on to the pitch to help an injured player, tripped over and broke a bottle of chloroform he was carrying. The fumes knocked him out and stretchermen had to carry him back to the dressing room to sleep it off.

Graham Smith was goalkeeper for Notts County, Colchester, West Brom and Cambridge and had a habit of kicking the goal posts for luck before the game started. One day he followed his usual routine while playing for Colchester and went to his right post and kicked it. Then he went to his left post and kicked it. Then the crossbar fell down and knocked him out!

When Steve Bull left school he never thought he would one day be a professional so, like most school-leavers, he hunted for a job. But where did he get his first job? In a bedding factory! Since then he has stopped many a goalkeeper from keeping a clean sheet!

Back in 1936, York City were so keen to sign talented teenager George Lee that their officials waited outside his house until midnight struck to herald in his 17th birthday. They were then legally able to sign him. He was exactly 17 years and 30 seconds when the ink dried.

Don't be surprised if you see French goalie Bernard Lama wearing some strange socks. The Paris St. Germain star, who is No.1 choice for France, gets someone to buy him a pair of the opposition's socks before each match so that he can wear them below his own socks during the game. He believes it brings him luck.

"Oooh! That's it, Dennis! Scratch just there!"

nick **BARMBY**

a county practice!

Stockport's ALUN ARMSTRONG has an unusual way of keeping fit!

LAST SEASON Geordie striker Alun Armstrong and his Stockport County team-mates captured the nation's hearts with a giant-killing Coca-Cola Cup run.

Alun carried an ankle injury for most of the season, but still played his part in the momentous cup victories over Blackburn Rovers, West Ham and Southampton.

However, more important for the Edgeley Park side was their end-of-season promotion to the First Division, a feat which takes Alun another step closer to fulfilling a prophecy made to him by former Newcastle boss, Kevin Keegan.

Says Alun, "I was a Newcastle player as a teenager and it was my dream to play first-team football and win trophies with them.

"But during the summer of 1994, when I was 19 years old, Kevin told me that my prospects would be better if I left and tried for first-team football elsewhere.

"He assured me that it wasn't a question of them needing money and that I didn't have to go.

"But he was planning to to bring in some big-name strikers and he thought it unlikely that I would get first-team football in the near future. 'Go out and make a name for yourself,' he advised.

"With hindsight, it was the best advice I could have had. Stockport gave me the chance of senior football and my game has improved immensely.

"I also realise now that I would never have been given a look-in at Newcastle had I stayed. At the time, however, I resented being pushed out. Newcastle was my team and I didn't want to leave.

"But Kevin was thinking of my future and it was the best thing he could have done for me. Last season was fantastic and now I'll be getting a chance to prove myself in the First Division."

Alun hit the back of the

net 13 times last term, not a prolific record but one made all the more remarkable by an amazing injury problem.

Explains Alun, "After each game my ankle would swell up and I had to go through the bizarre routine of sitting in front of the television with my foot in a bucket of ice.

"Our physio, Rodger Wylde, devised an exercise for me to do each Sunday. I wrapped a rubber strap around both ankles and continuously pulled one leg away from each other in different directions.

"Rodger told me that the exercise would, in the long run, help to strengthen the ligament.

"During the week, while the rest of the lads were playing five-a-side, he had me hopping up the steps in Edgeley Park's main stand on one leg.

"After half an hour of that, I was absolutely shattered.

"When I first arrived at the club, Rodger was quick to tell me that he thought I had weak ankles and devised those special routines for me to strengthen them.

"It seemed to work, and I just carried on as normal afterwards.

"Now I realise that I may have to revert to those exercises and keep doing them for the rest of my career as a precaution." ●

stop him!
(ANY WAY YOU CAN!)

TOPICAL TIMES FOOTBALL BOOK **1998**

TOPICAL TIMES FOO...

B

➤ SHOT 1

➤ SHOT 2

TOPICAL TIMES FOOTBALL BOOK **1998**

TOPICAL TIMES FOOTBALL BOO...

C

➤ SHOT 1

➤ SHOT 2

➤ SHOT 2

➤ SHOT 3

➤ SHOT 3

A

Newcastle United's Faustino Asprilla, blocked by Coventry City's Brian Borrows.

B

Didier Deschamps, Juventus, brings Manchester United's David Beckham to a halt.

C

Asprilla (again). This time Coventry's Dion Dublin is the culprit.

homedraw

DISNEY'S favourite cartoon characters became an obsession for Ian Bishop the day he started to decorate his young son Jordan's bedroom.

Starting with Snow White and the Seven Dwarfs, the West Ham midfielder began to fill every available wall with colourful images of some of the best-known animated stars of the cinema. He'd be up all hours with a paintbrush in his hand.

Then, when he'd finished one room, he moved next door to do the same for his younger boy, Connor. The results are stunning but they could all change at any time.

"As the boys get older, they'll get interested in other things," says Ian. "Star Wars could be my next big project.

"I've loved the Star Wars films ever since they first came out. Jordan loves them too.

"It was great fun doing the Disney characters. I got so into it that I used to rush back from training with West Ham every day to get started on the painting.

"It was much more fun than wall-papering. I've never been any good at that.

"My wife Jane would just bring me cups of tea and I'd go on painting for hours and hours. People always say footballers have too much time on their hands, well I was making the most of mine.

"The first picture I did was of Snow White and the Dwarfs. It came from a book that Jane had enjoyed when she was a kid.

"There were one of two scary things like the wicked witch and a castle that I left out of the scene. I didn't want Jordan to be frightened by it when he woke up.

"Instead I put in a few birds and things that he would like. I wanted something to fill as much of the wall as possible.

"After I'd finished the Snow White picture, I started to do more characters on the other walls. Mickey Mouse and Winnie the Pooh both get a good show."

Ian's West Ham team-mates knew nothing about his pictures until they were featured on Sky Sports. After that he started to get a few requests.

"Sky had just come to interview me before one of the live games," says Ian. "But when they saw the Disney pictures, they want to film them as well.

"We were away in a hotel when it was shown but manager Harry Redknapp's wife came in and said she'd seen my little boy on the television. After that Steve Potts' wife asked me to do a picture for their little boy as well.

"Painting is something I've always enjoyed, ever since I was a kid. In fact, art was probably the only thing I enjoyed at school.

"I'm just sorry now I didn't concentrate harder on my exams. The problem was I already knew I was going to be an apprentice at Everton and that was a big distraction.

"Over the years I've kept up with a bit of sketching, including one or two drawings of team-mates. When I first joined West Ham I drew Stuart Slater and Frank McAvennie

and my efforts were auctioned for charity.

"I'm not the only footballer who draws a bit either. Liverpool's David James made a name for himself with his pictures when he was a

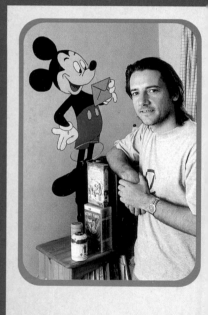

116

VS!

Ian Bishop!

young 'keeper at Watford.

"It's a great way to forget all about football. When you're playing twice a week in our game, you need to relax and painting is just the job for me." ●

117

SHEFFIELD WEDNESDAY **peter** ATHERTON

who'd be a ref?

You can forgive Scottish Grade One referee Bobby Orr for feeling the pace. He's just finished a rigorous fitness test run by the Scottish Football Association. The pace of today's game demands a strict level of fitness for the men in the middle, and regular fitness checks are held to make sure the referees are up to the mark.

So, if you think referees aren't fit, why don't YOU try running 50 metres in 6.9 seconds, 200 metres in 28.4 seconds and 3,000 metres in twelve minutes? Or ask Bobby Orr what it's like!

"and today's

With all the cloak and dagger secrecy employed by managers nowadays, usually the earliest fans find out how their teams will line up is over the tannoy five minutes before kick-off.

The match day magazine tries vainly to predict the tactical line-ups employed by the respective managers, but there's more to a programme than that. It's a magazine crammed with information, news, views and statistics. All this doesn't happen by accident, though. Behind each programme there is a team of enthusiastic researchers and designers, all eager to bring you the best content possible.

The "Topical Times" popped into La Rive Productions, London, where it was all go on the deadline day for the F.A. Cup Semi-Final programmes.

1 Every programme needs player profiles of each team, and with over 70 players likely to feature in the semi-final squads, that's some job. Editor Ian Vosper gets down to work!

4 Lay-out of the pages is in the capable hands of designer Tony Kett.

7 . . . . before they are folded and stapled under the watchful eye of Ivan Whitehead.

2 Action from previous matches is also an important ingredient of the programmes. Goals that got the teams there and so on. checks the picture quality closely.

3 Ian hands over the details to computer designer Barry Stevens.

5 The work is finished and ready for printing. There's no time to lose and a fast car is ready to head to the printing H.Q.

6 Hot off the press. Mick Milborrow checks the first proofs . . .

■ Match-day programme collecting is popular with fans of all ages and the official Football Programme Directory numbers over 1000 members. Programmes can be cherished souvenirs of famous Cup victories, championship deciders — or a 6-0 win over your greatest rivals!

Old programmes can often be worth a considerable sum of money. Check your attic — or your dad's or grandad's . . . someone, somewhere could be sitting on a fortune!

8 And this is where they end up. Programme, sir?

9 The La Rive staff take a well-earned breather. Tony, Managing Director Colum Fitzgerald, Ian and Barry.

121

the wemb

...and this time it's a winning one for Crystal Palace's CARLO NASH!

CARLO NASH banished a Wembley nightmare when he anchored Crystal Palace to First Division play-off victory over Sheffield United last season.

Goalkeeper Nash returned to the national stadium just twelve months after the biggest disappointment of his life, to help Palace regain their Premiership status.

Nash had tasted bitter FA Vase Final defeat with non-league Clitheroe at the hands of Brigg Town. Yet even that 3-0 reverse had a happy ending, because his Wembley performance impressed scouts from Crystal Palace.

By the start of last season, Nash had joined Palace for £35,000 and his career was close to completing a dramatic circle.

As a youngster, Carlo was spotted by Manchester United, where he joined Ryan Giggs in the School of Excellence. Four years at Old Trafford left the 'keeper on the brink of a professional career with United.

But then came disaster. Nash was involved in a nasty car crash with his mother and ended up turning his back on football.

"It was an awful shock," says Carlo. "I wasn't hurt physically, but I lost all my confidence and my interest in football.

"Instead I decided to concentrate on my schoolwork. There were exams to think about, which suddenly seemed more important than football.

"It was only later, when I went to college, that I started to play football again.Even then, it was only for a pub team, the Waterworks Tavern in Bacup.

"But I began to get noticed again. I joined Rossendale, and then Clitheroe. At the time I was working as a sales manager for a company in Clitheroe, training on Thursday nights, and playing on a Saturday.

"It all changed again with the run we had to the FA Vase final. I heard that a few clubs were watching me.

"Even so, I was amazed to hear that Palace were keen, especially as Dave Bassett had never seen me play. I was really enjoying life at Clitheroe, but when the crunch comes, you have to follow your ambitions.

"I wasn't expecting a lot when I joined Crystal Palace. Even though Nigel Martyn had just left for Leeds, I knew I was basically there as number two.

"What I had to do was adapt quickly, and learn fast. That seemed to happen, and by February I had managed to force my way into the first team ahead of England Under-21 'keeper Chris Day.

"It didn't take me long to get used to professional football. It's a lot easier than working full-time, and training in the evenings!

"I've even done some modelling work with team-mate Dougie Freedman. Obviously football comes first, but it's a bit of fun and some extra money.

"I've got something to fall back on when things are quiet. A lot of players do it these days.

"Getting back to Wembley for the play-off final was incredible. The atmosphere was fantastic. I hope I can get there again.

"Playing at Wembley is out of this

> **I wasn't expecting a lot when I joined Crystal Palace.**

● Carlo in action for Palace in the Wembley play-off final v. Sheffield United.

ley way

world. The playing surface is so good.

"We've had some problems with our own pitch at Selhurst Park. Because of the number of matches played there, it lost a lot of grass, and towards the end of the season was very hard and bobbly.

"It's our home ground, and you can't keep making excuses. But it was great for the players to play Sheffield United on a pitch that allowed them to knock the ball around.

"When David Hopkin's winning goal went in it made up for all the disappointment of last year's defeat for me with Clitheroe, and for rest of the lads the play-off defeat by Leicester.

"Now it's incredible to be in the Premiership, and in the position of being able to play at Old Trafford.

"Being at United as a kid was fantastic for me. It's great to be able to show them how I have progressed since then." ●

picture list

(A) ALBERTZ, *Jorg.* 75
ANDERTON, *Darren.* 61
ARMSTRONG, *Alun.* 113
ATHERTON, *Peter.* 118

(B) BARMBY, *Nick.* 112
BATTY, *David.*10
BISHOP, *Ian.* 116
BJORKLUND *Joachim.* 78
BOWYER, *Lee.* 68
BRADBURY, *Lee.* 48
BRIGHTWELL, *Ian.* 82

(C) COLLINS, *John.* 102
CROSSLEY, *Mark.* 76

(D) DODDS, *Billy.* 52

(E) EARLE, *Robbie.* 124

(F) FOWLER, *Robbie.* 103

(G) GALLACHER, *Kevin.* 94
GEMMELL, *Tommy* 92
GRAY, *Michael.* 23

(H) HATELEY, *Mark.* 90
HENDRIE, *John.* 62
HESKEY, *Emile.* 54
HIGNETT, *Craig.* 104
HODDLE, *Glenn.* 72
HUCKERBY, *Darren.* 43
HUGHES, *Michael.* 17
HUGHES, *Mark.* 96

(I) IVERSEN, *Steffen.* 28
IZZET, *Muzzy* .16

(K) KEANE, *Roy.* 74

(L) LEBOEUF, *Frank.* 32

(M) McALLISTER, *Gary.* 22
McATEER, *Jason.* 12
McKINLAY, *Tosh.* 35
MARTYN, *Nigel.* 44
MUSTOE, *Robbie.* 41

(N) NASH, *Carlo.* 122
NEWSOME, *Jon.* 88

(O) OSTENSTADT, *Egil.* 26

(P) PEDERSEN, *Per.* 36
PLATT, *David.* 18
POLLOCK, *Jamie.* 107
POWELL, *Darryl.* 40

(R) REUTER, *Stefan.* 55
ROBERTO CARLOS. 67

(S) SAUNDERS, *Dean.* 85
SCHMEICHEL, *Peter.* 6
SCIMECA, *Riccardo.* 25
SHEARER, *Alan.* 64, 95
SHORT, *Craig.* 30
SOUTHGATE, *Gareth.* 80
STUBBS, *Alan.* 20
STURRIDGE, *Dean.* 100
SULLIVAN, *Neil.* 50

(V) VIEIRA, *Patrick.* 9

(Z) ZOLA, *Gianfranco.* 60

model
professionals

Batty

Hendry

Le Saux

Townsend

Schmeichel

Cruyff